Dedication

To James, my husband, my best friend,
my love, my life. For all your
encouragement and for
always believing in me.
Thank you.
I love you.

To Jeff,
I had a great time with you on the tour! Thank you!

Inside the Shelton Gang

One Daughter's Discovery

[handwritten signature] 5-14-16

By RUTHIE SHELTON
Daughter of 'Little Carl' Shelton
and grand-niece of the infamous Shelton Brothers

and JON MUSGRAVE
Southern Illinois historian and co-author
of Secrets of the Herrin Gangs

Published by
IllinoisHistory.com
PO Box 1142
Marion IL 62959

Front Cover
"Little Carl" Shelton and his car, as well as Carl Shelton's mug shots from Leavenworth Penitentiary.

Back Cover
Ruthie Shelton on the beach at Jacksonville, Florida. *Andre Giauque photographer.*

Cover Design
Jon Musgrave

Library of Congress Control Number: 2013905093

International Standard Book Number (ISBN)
paperback: 978-0-9707984-8-0

Printed in the United States of America

3rd printing

Chapter 1.

The Big Reveal

"I've been kidnapped!"

Pop's voice was low and raspy, "They've got me tied up. I'm on a dock. You've got to come and get me."

This was the voice on the other end of the phone every night after I got home from a long, exhausting day, sitting at my dad's bedside in the hospital. As soon as I got in my house the phone would ring and the nurse would say, "You have to try and calm your dad down." The nurse put the phone to his ear and the same conversation would be repeated night after night.

I would watch the sun rise in my rear view mirror as I drove away from my home on Black Hammock Island in Jacksonville on Florida's Atlantic coast every morning. Scenes of orange and yellow filled the sky with a peaceful, calming, feeling. But what I was headed for had no peacefulness or calmness about it. My destination was like driving into hurricane force winds. For all of my life this had been my home. I was born and raised among these palm trees and sand dunes. My roots sank deep here, or so I thought. Trees in shallow soil don't fare well in storms. The storm still raged in that bed and what it would reveal would shake me to my core.

Driving back to the hospital each day I hoped I would find my dad awake and alert. It wrenched my heart to see him in that hospital bed. His tanned skin turned pale and his baby blues lacked their luster and vibrancy. He could see, but just not me. He wasn't blind, but he didn't see what was actually there. In his mind he had gone back to a different place and time. He saw people as clearly as if they were standing in front of him, but they weren't. He saw places he hadn't been to in over 50 years, just as real as if he were standing there today.

Pop, as we call my dad, had barely survived surgery and now he didn't know where he was. He kept trying to get out of the bed, to "escape" as he would say. The doctors had to keep him strapped down for his own safety. "You have to get me out of here," he said repeatedly. I kept trying to tell him that he had to stay in the hospital bed but he didn't understand, "No. They're trying to kill us. We have to go, now!"

Every time I left the room he would call out for me, "Ruthie, get me out of here! Somebody get my daughter. Get Ruthie!"

Thus began a week of incoherent ramblings and delusions. There were to be revelations that would forever change my life and change who I am. These unexpected disclosures would answer questions about my own life that I had long since given up on ever knowing the truth about. A course of events was about to unfold that would bring Pop's life full circle. The drugs that had relaxed his body for surgery had broken through decades-old barriers and cautions. The anesthesia had left him temporarily living in the past, his past, a past I knew nothing about. He was now about to inadvertently share with me the life he had left behind a half century before. Most importantly, the end result would reunite him with his first daughter, my sister, Elaine, after a lifetime apart!

I was born into a war that I never knew existed. I was protected, sheltered, hidden, even trained. My mother's instructions to me were, "always check for wires before opening the front door of the house." No explanation was given. I had learned to ask no questions. I did as I was told. I now know that she lived in fear my whole life, fear for her safety, terror for mine. This fear escalated, especially after she and my dad were divorced. When I was 15 my mother told me she had papers drawn up to "give me away." It didn't seem to me that it mattered where I went as long as it was "away." And I didn't know why. But it never happened. My dad stepped in and made sure I was okay.

This was a war that was supposed to have ended in 1951. It played out in the Midwest. The town was named Fairfield, not a name you would expect for the story that was about to be told to me. Fairfield lies in Wayne County, Illinois. By that time, only one side would show themselves openly, the other would be identified by police, sheriffs and the FBI, as "person or persons unknown." This war continued beyond the deaths of all the major players and affected, touched, shaped, even controlled the lives of the next generation, and, unfortunately, the one to follow – mine.

It was the winter of 2003, Pop had been feeling excessively tired. He had no energy at all, he just wanted to sleep all the time. I just thought it was because he was getting older. He liked to tell people he was "going on 80 years old." This was the opposite of how he had lived his life up until the last year or so. He was always busy, running around with his grandchildren, taking care of his animals, working in the yard, helping his neighbors with whatever project they had going, he just never sat still. He was always the first to be ready when there was a trip to take. Over the years he traveled across the country and back with me and my family, many times.

The news from the doctor was crushing to me, Pop needed to have his heart valve replaced. Open heart surgery was required! I didn't think it was a good idea to have such an extensive surgery at 79 years old. But Pop faced this surgery as he lived his life. He hit the problem head on. He never hesitated, "Let's do it!" he told the doctor.

The arrangements were made and all too quickly the day of the surgery came. Pop was very optimistic. He was sure this operation would return him to the life he had always lived. I didn't want him to have the surgery. I was so afraid it would turn out badly. After all, I'd rather have the tired Pop with us than lose him, even if he couldn't do the things he had always loved. But I never told him how I felt. It was his decision to make and I didn't want to influence him.

As we sat in the surgical waiting room in the hospital the hours drug by. Pop's girlfriend and companion of 20 years, Nell, sat nervously by me. "The woman who tamed Pop" is what we call her. Pop was always popular with the ladies. After he and my mother divorced he had a different girlfriend every time I turned around, usually he had two girlfriends at a time. The one he was dating openly and one on the side, "just in case," as Pop would say. Usually, the "one on the side" had money, a lot of money. His woman chasing days ended after he met Nell. Pop's "Nell" was the only lady in his life from then on, he loved her.

My husband, James, was there with me. We have been married since January 1977, and have four children together, Missi, J.C., (James Carl), Jenny and Krystin. Waiting for news in a hospital is never easy and they tried to keep the mood light. Someone pulled out a deck of cards. Never in my life has a family member been in the hospital that card playing wasn't involved. Cards were dealt, flipped and thrown down. Food and drinks came and went. As the morning turned into afternoon no distraction was enough to keep me from feeling that something was terribly wrong.

Every time the doors of the waiting room opened I jumped to my feet hoping that it was Pop's surgeon. But time and again it wasn't. Other families were awaiting news just like we were, and their doctors' came in, gave them their updates and left. And we sat waiting. Watching the clock on the wall, it seemed the hands never moved. I had the ominous feeling that my life was about to take a dramatic change, little did I know how dramatic it would be!

Recently, as I was putting the finishing touches on my book, I realized that some of my memories of that day are a little blurred. So I returned to Memorial Hospital in Jacksonville to try and relive what I could from that day. It's amazing what the sights, sounds and smells of an experience can bring back to the memory.

I parked at the nearby bank, as I did every day Pop was a patient there. It was easier than the hospital parking garage, that seemed too confining. I walked across the parking lot as I did all those days ago. I walked through the entrance to the hospital, spoke to the dear little ladies at the information desk, and walked, very slowly, toward the coronary waiting room. I didn't know exactly what to expect. But through this whole experience, I haven't known what to expect and everything that has happened, to me, to Pop, has so exceeded anything I could ever have imagined!

As I walked into the waiting room, I was greeted by the hospital patient liaison person. He explained to me that he is the person who intercedes between the doctor and the patient's family. This would have been the liaison who let us know when Pop was put on the bypass machine which worked for his heart and lungs during the surgery. He said to me, "I love my job. It's great!"

I told him why I was there. My dad had open heart surgery a few years ago and revealed his hidden past to me as he regained consciousness, after being unconscious for five days. I told him I was writing a book about my dad's family and my experience of discovering all about his past. He told me to take all the time I needed.

The waiting room was large and open. It was quiet, except for the TV showing local news and weather. How much louder it must have been the day my family was there waiting for news of Pop. I could hear the coffee machine running in the background, I could smell the aroma. It reminded me of just how much coffee I drank the day of Pop's surgery and the days of waiting to follow.

One little, older lady sat there alone. This reminded me of Nell. This lady wore tan slacks and a cream colored blouse with a matching sweater. Her hair was cut similar to Nell's. I wondered who she was waiting to hear about. If it was the love of her life like Nell was waiting to hear about hers. I felt so bad for this lady, waiting alone. I could hear people talking and laughter in the distance. There was no laughter the day I waited to hear about Pop, if there was, I didn't hear it.

This day I looked around at the nice furnishings, something I definitely wouldn't have noticed before. The pictures hanging on the walls are of palm trees and coconuts in a beach scene. Some are of the Florida wetlands with egrets taking flight in front of the palm trees. Quite appropriate for living so close to the beach.

As I left the waiting room, I stopped to thank the liaison.

"I've already googled your name and read some about your family," he told me.

I felt a chill go down my spine. Even at this late stage of the writing process, the words Pop had long engraved in my brain, were still echoing in my ears, "Don't let 'em know who you are!"

I remember back to the day of Pop's surgery. Finally Pop's doctor walked through those waiting room doors. The look on his face told me my worries were valid. My heart dropped. I felt all the blood drain from my face. I was sick to my stomach. As the surgeon sat down across from our family, James took my hand. The doctor explained that it had been a very difficult surgery. They had almost lost Pop, but he was a fighter.

He had survived! The waiting room was filled with cheering as our fears turned to thankfulness. The doctor said as soon as Pop was out of recovery Nell and I could go in and see him.

Now we just had to wait for him to wake up. Hours turned into days as Nell and I sat by his side in the I.C.U. Pop looked so weak laying there in that hospital bed. He was hooked up to tubes and wires and the room was cold, so very cold. I wished I had told him how I felt about him having this surgery. If I had told him I didn't want him to have it maybe he would have changed his mind, maybe he wouldn't be laying in this hospital bed now. He could be at home watching the birds eat out of their bird feeders in front of his window. While we were waiting, Nell told me she didn't want Pop to have the surgery either. But she didn't speak up for the same reasons as me, it was his life, his choice, his decision to make.

Nurses were in and out of his room seemingly every couple of minutes checking on him. He was unconscious for five grueling days.

"Why isn't he waking up?" I would ask. I got so many different answers.

"People react differently to surgery."

"Some take longer to wake up than others."

Nobody seemed to really know what was going on. We were so worried. Finally the doctor told us exactly why Pop was still out, "He had a bad reaction to the anesthesia."

There was no way to know when he would wake up or what condition he would be in when, or even if he woke up.

Sitting at his bedside for those days, I had a lot of time to reflect on my life growing up. I was born in Jacksonville, Florida, June 19, 1960. Pop married my mother, Elsie Lee Duffie, in the 1950s. She was from Georgia, growing up picking cotton as a child. Pop worked as a carpenter, mostly in Atlanta or Miami. He had a long way to travel every week. On Monday morning he would leave our home in Jacksonville, sometimes as early as 2 a.m. to drive to work. He would spend the week there working but as soon as he got off on Fridays he headed straight home to spend the weekend with my older brother and me. I remember as a little girl him telling me the only reason he came home every weekend was to spend time with "you kids."

Once he was so tired he fell asleep while driving home. A police officer came up behind him and seeing Pop's car swerving on the road, he knew the driver must be asleep at the wheel. The officer started flashing his lights at him. Pop woke up and safely pulled over. The officer said he could tell Pop was asleep driving down the road. He kept flashing his lights hoping to wake him without startling him so he wouldn't have a wreck.

One thing we loved doing together was riding our motorcycles. There was an old abandoned airport nearby and we spent Saturdays there with other motorcycle riders. This place was so cool. There were runways that the airplanes once taxied down. It was surrounded by woods so there were a lot of trails to ride and my favorite thing was all the tall sand dunes to climb on our bikes. There were also a lot of "No Trespassing" signs that we ignored. The police would come out about once every six months and run all of us off. We would leave that weekend. The next weekend we would all be back!

We would race down the runways. "Slow down!" Pop would yell from his Yamaha, knowing I was not slowing down that little Honda I rode for anything. He taught me to drive a stick shift Volkswagen at that old airport when I was only 9 years old. Sometimes we took our dune buggy out there to drive it all over the sand dunes.

My greatest love was and is the beach. Whether it was Jacksonville Beach or Little Talbot Island, I loved the sand and the surf. I remember one time Pop was about to get fined because I was playing around in the sea oats. It was illegal, but somehow he talked his way out of it.

Oh, yeah, and we had guns, always, lots of guns. On the wall in the house, in the closet, in the car, in the garage, in my dad's belt, there were guns everywhere. It seems every day we spent together we would pull out the guns and practice shooting targets, cans, bottles and sometimes we would end up at the shooting range. I, of course, thought this was how everyone grew up and, at the time, I thought it was all just for fun. .

By the time I was a teenager Pop worked in town some. Occasionally he would pick me up after school and we'd go to the pool hall and shoot a few games. I never knew Pop to gamble, but I also never knew anyone who could beat him. Pool, cards, it didn't matter what the game was, Pop always won.

Of all my memories of my father the ones I treasure the most involve my friends. Pop took us everywhere we wanted to go, did whatever we wanted to do. He even took me and my friends to the Gator Bowl to see the football games. We all piled into Pop's Firebird, a bunch of laughing, silly, teenage boys and girls and he loved it, so did we. I remember one game we went to, Pop decided he wanted to beat all the traffic home, so we had to leave just before the game was over. Our team was ahead when we left, so by the time we got out to the car and heard all the cheering, we thought the game was over and we had won. After Pop dropped my friends off, and then he dropped me off at home, I found out the cheering was for the other team, they had scored when we left and they won! I never let Pop live that down, we laughed about it so many times over the years.

Of course when I was a kid I didn't fully appreciate all Pop did for me and what he went through to be with me. My parents separated when I was young, about six years old as I remember, but Pop made sure that he stayed a constant part of my life. Then they divorced when I was a teenager. That was when my mother really started obsessing over our safety.

I knew checking for wires on the front door was a little bizarre but it was easier to go along with what she wanted than to argue with her every time I came home. She didn't even want me to walk to the mailbox, and when I did, "never stand in front of the mailbox to open it," she would say, "there could be a bomb."

At that time in my life I had no idea why this was going on or what could make my mother act the way she did. Through my whole life, any time things did not go well for my mother, she always had the same threat to make, "I'll slit my wrists." Some parts of my childhood were very difficult. Eventually her mental health was affected for the worse.

There was one part of our life where Pop had a wall between us – his past. I never knew anything about my dad's past, where he came from, where he was born, how he got to be who he was. I never got to hear stories of him growing up, his school days, the time he spent in the navy. I knew nothing about my grandparents or where they came from or even if they were still alive. There was no asking questions, no researching, no trying to find out about his past – ever. It just wasn't allowed! I always felt like I just landed on this earth with no history, no background, no roots.

Once in high school I had an opportunity to write articles for the *Jacksonville Journal*. When they published my first one I came home so proud and excited. I had my first byline! I just knew my parents were going to be so proud of me. After all, I had been writing stories all my life, and that's all I ever wanted to be, a Pulitzer Prize winning writer! But I didn't get the reaction I expected. My parents hit the roof! I was *not allowed* to have my name in the newspaper. There was no explanation given, that was just how it was. So I did what any good, obedient daughter would do – I wrote under a pseudonym.

The next time I had a story published in the newspaper the reaction was completely different. Pop was so proud of me. He took me to see a friend of his that I had never met before. We met him in a restaurant. Pop introduced me as "My daughter, the writer," and showed the man the newspaper. The man read my story, critiqued it, and gave me some pointers for writing. I always thought there was something kind of strange about that meeting, but I knew not to question anything. I've never forgotten that day but I still don't know who that man was.

Another time in high school when I felt like an alien from another planet was when I was assigned to write a genealogy paper. I really went rounds with my parents over that, and as good as Pop was to me he still had a temper and he was stubborn, very stubborn. In the end Pop's side was left blank.

Once though, for a split second, I caught a glimpse into Pop's past, a very brief, yet painful glimpse. When I was a small child I found a picture of an adorable little girl. She had blonde hair and blue eyes and she was wearing a party dress with white lace socks

Ruthie Shelton collection

MYSTERY PHOTO – The "princess" turned out to be the author's older sister Elaine Shelton.

and patent leather shoes. I thought she must have been a princess! I took the picture to my mother and made the horrible mistake of asking the question, "Who is this?" I was told, "This is your father's *first* daughter, Elaine!" The picture was snatched from my fingers, and that was the end of that conversation – for good.

I had a sister and although I couldn't know her or even ask any questions about her, I knew she was out there. That episode in my life gave me the hope that there was someone in the world like me, someone who could understand what I thought, how I felt. It would be many years before I would find out how very alike Elaine and I really are. After that glimpse into Pop's past, the picture of my sister disappeared and the wall closing off the world my father knew before was never breached again.

After five long days of Pop laying in that hospital bed lifeless, he started to mumble some words. At first I couldn't understand anything he said, but it didn't matter, I had hope that he was going to be alright. I thought he was wanting to know where he was, what had happened to him. So I would try to reassure him that he had surgery but was going to be fine. When he was a little clearer and I could understand him better it seemed very strange the words he managed to communicate with me – shooting, liquor, cash, guns – not what you would expect someone coming out of major surgery to be concerned with.

Then he started making the motions of drawing a gun and shooting. He'd say, "There they are. Over there!" and he would draw, his fingers making the shape of a gun, and start firing. When I'd ask what he was doing he would say, "We have to get them. We can't let them get away." I got the idea he wasn't shooting cans off a fence post! "They" were on the ceiling, by the TV, coming in the door. Then he would pull me down close to him and say, very quietly, "Don't let them know who you are. They can't find us. Don't let them find us!"

Then there were the stacks of imaginary money he was counting out. He was so specific in his movements you could tell exactly what he was doing. He'd count the bills, lick his thumb, count some more, and tie them into bundles. It was all like he'd done it many times before, only for real.

I would stay as late as I could every day but as soon as I got home the nurses would call. "You've got to calm your dad down," they would say. They would put the phone to his ear.

"It's me, Pop, it's Ruthie," I'd try to calm him down, "you're in the hospital, you had surgery but you're going to be fine."

"I've been kidnapped. They've got me tied up. I'm on a dock. You've got to come and get me."

This went on night after night. Reasoning with him didn't help. In his brain he was tied up on a dock and waiting for me to rescue him.

"Are you okay. Pop?" I would ask him.

"Yes, I'm okay, but you've got to come get me."

It was the same thing over and over. I finally found the only thing that would calm him down was if I asked, "Is there a bed there? Are you comfortable?" He would say yes, there was a bed and he was comfortable. "Then you stay in the bed and I'll be there first thing in the morning to get you." After that conversation he would calm down and go to sleep.

As time passed and the anesthesia wore out of his system he started to make more sense. I walked into his hospital room on the sixth day after his surgery and he was sitting up in the bed with a smile on his face. "What took you so long to get here?" he asked me with a laugh. He knew he was in the hospital and that he had surgery. Everything was getting back to normal. Everything except for the stories he was telling me of a past life that couldn't possibly be true; always with a warning not to let anyone know who I am or where he was.

I was beginning to hear of a life my dad had lived many years before my birth, a life that seemed to include fast cars, liquor, guns and an incredible amount of money. Much of this he told me in a matter of fact, light hearted sort of way. "One day I..." seemed to be the beginning of many sentences, but when he started telling me about his family it was a different kind of story. There was a certain sadness that came over him as he told me of the uncle he was named after, Big Carl. His voice was still raspy but he was determined to tell me about his uncle. I leaned close over Pop to hear every word. He told me all about a pivotal day in his life. It was the last time his Uncle Carl would drive his Jeep through a place called the "Pond Creek Bottoms."

It was a place in the Midwest that I had never heard of. But I would later find it to be an area so untouched by time the pages on the calendar rarely turn. Where the moon shines so brightly on the hills you can lay in the grass and count every star in heaven while the lightening bugs twinkle and dance above you. On a clear night you can watch deer graze freely on the open land as the deafening silence is broken only by the howling of the coyote in the distance. A land where the secrets run as deep as the river that is rumored to run beneath it.

Pop got so upset as he was telling me that Uncle Carl always picked him up to ride with him in Pond Creek, tears started to roll down his face. But he didn't pick him up that day.

"Why didn't he come by and get me? Why?" Pop would say over and over. "Uncle Carl was in his Jeep alone."

Pop said his uncle usually drove bullet-proof cars but not when he went out to his farmland. Then his favorite ride was his World War II army issue Jeep. I tried to calm Pop down, thinking all the time, "Who are you?" Then Pop would strain to continue his story. I'd ask him to wait and tell me when he was stronger and feeling better. He would get so frustrated.

"No, no, you have to listen!" he'd plead. So I'd listened.

It was October 23, 1947, a beautiful, cool fall morning, as Pop described it. Big Carl owned farmland in Pond Creek, just five miles southeast of Fairfield, in Wayne County, Illinois. Pop's brother, Little Earl (named after Pop's other uncle, Big Earl) and Ray Walker, a friend and employee of Pop's uncles, followed in a pickup truck. As he drove down that dirt and gravel road, Big Carl was ambushed by gunfire. His Jeep swerved as his body was hit by bullets from a rifle, a revolver and a machine gun. The shots came from the bushes beside the road as he approached a bridge. He came out of his Jeep firing the pearl handled revolver Pop said his uncle always carried.

As he returned fire, Uncle Carl was out gunned and outnumbered. He had only one bullet left as he fell face down into the ditch, landing on his gun. There would be one more barrage of bullets, fired into a man who lay dead or dying. Then, silence. The gunfire stopped and the shooters fled the scene.

Pop felt that if he had been there he could have made a difference. I said, "Pop, if you had been there you would have been killed too!"

I didn't know where this Pond Creek was or why his Uncle Carl was murdered in such a heinous way, in broad daylight, but I could tell it was very important to Pop that I take in every word he was revealing to me, and I did. The authorities determined that Uncle Carl was murdered by "person or persons unknown." This was the first strike in the war between my family and the "unknown assailants" that would haunt the rest of their lives.

Pop continued to reveal to me the past he held in such secret that his closest friends never suspected, a past that he lived in dread of being discovered, a life he had to leave behind for his safety and the safety of all those he loved, including his first daughter. He told me how he and the surviving members of his family fled Southern Illinois in 1951 to began life again in Jacksonville, Florida.

My dad, now called Pop by all who loved him, was "Little Carl" Shelton of the "Shelton Gang," referred to by the *Saturday Evening Post* as the "Bloodiest Gang in America."

Chapter 2.
Who are You People?

Soon, Pop was getting stronger every day. And every day he had a new story to tell me. He told me about when he and his brother, Little Earl, were kids in Pond Creek in the 1930s, they would go up to Tondini Hill, called this after the owner, Mickal Tondini. He was an Italian immigrant, coming from Tirol Province, Austria, arriving in America in 1902, barely speaking English. He was a farmer but his great love was making wine. Pop and Little Earl wanted some of this wine for their own to drink. Those kids would take their dog with them and trade him for a quart of wine. Then the boys would run back down the hill as fast as they could go, with their wine in hand, and whistle for their dog. I can only imagine that sweet old man laughing as he watched that dog running back to those boys. Then they would find a very large tree to sit under with their old dog and sip their homemade wine.

How Pop and I would laugh as he told me his happy childhood memories. These were the stories I missed out on when I was growing up. Now Pop was finally sharing them with me. After all these years of living my life with no history, I was so happy that he wanted to tell me about his past. Happy, but also very confused and very, very angry. Not angry at Pop, well maybe just a little, but mostly angry at the situation. I really couldn't be mad at Pop, every time he started opening up to me about his past, I could see how painful it all was for him. Still the fact remains that through my whole life I was never told one single thing about Pop's family. I could understand not telling me when I was a child, but I was grown with a family of my own. Why couldn't I be told after I was grown?

The big question in my mind was, if Pop wasn't who he was supposed to be, does that make me not who I always thought I was? That's the confusing part. My brain was spinning, I was trying to take in and remember everything Pop was telling me, but it was too much all at once. A lifetime of memories and experiences flooded out of him in just a short span of time. I started writing it all down so I wouldn't forget anything. The more he told me, the more questions I had. Who was this "Shelton Gang?" What did they do? Why did they have to leave their lives and homes in Illinois to start over again in Florida?

Pop told me they ran liquor in by boat from the Bahamas to St. Augustine, Florida. Then it was transferred to trucks and driven up to Jacksonville, then to Atlanta and right on into the Midwest; with Southern Illinois and St. Louis, Missouri being the destinations. The trucks had hollowed out seats, fake walls, anywhere liquor could be hidden it was. The cars and trucks had souped up engines to outrun the law. This was actually the birth of NASCAR, bootleggers outrunning police all through the south. So here it was, my family were bootleggers. But that was the least of what I was to find out over the next few months and years!

Pop was mostly concerned with me telling James about his past. "Don't tell James what I'm telling you," he would say to me. He loved James like his own son and was so worried that the truth would change his opinion of Pop. James loved Pop as a dad, and of course knowing about his past didn't change that.

"I have to tell him. I want to tell him. It's not going to change anything between you," I reassured him.

I also felt I had to tell my kids. My son and two of my daughters were grown by the time Pop told me who he really was and I would not have them feeling like I did – like I had been lied to my whole life. They had the same experiences as I did in school with genealogy assignments and they always wondered about their family tree but there was nothing I could tell them then. Pop constantly reminded me not to tell anyone who or where he was, his words still echo in my mind. But I made the decision to tell my kids and I swore them to secrecy. They were all thrilled to find out they had a heritage too. Whatever it was, it was better than never knowing anything about your family.

Most of the stories Pop shared with me were not pleasant. He told me how his Uncle Earl's house was bombed. Big Earl and his wife, Earline, lived in a very nice house in Pond Creek. At 3:00 a.m. they were jarred out of bed by the sound of glass breaking. They ran to the living room to find their large picture window broken. Before they realized what was happening a bomb exploded, blowing Earline backwards into the next room and setting the house on fire. The house burned to the ground before anyone could put out the flames. Sometime later their massive barn was set on fire, nothing was left of Big Earl Shelton's homestead.

Pop again warned me of the need to keep quiet about who and where we were, "The people who did those things are all dead by now," I told him.

"They have descendants," he would say.

I could only wonder why this sweet elderly couple had been the victims of such horrible violence.

Uncle Earl was the only one of Pop's uncles that I had actually known. Still I didn't get to know him until after I was grown. When I was growing up I was allowed to spend as much time with Pop as possible but I was not allowed to get to know or see any other Sheltons. I was told by a family member that when my cousins, Little Earl's kids, were little they were dropped off at my house all the time. They would stay for hours. But after about 1966-1967 that all changed. My uncles, aunts, or cousins no longer came to my house and I didn't get to know any of the Shelton family, except Pop, until after I was grown.

. In the spring of 1966, March or April, Pop made a phone call to Fairfield, Illinois. He wanted to see his little girl, Elaine. The daughter he had not seen since she was just a little baby girl. Now she was a teenager, a junior in high school, all grown up. He wouldn't blame Elaine if she refused to see him. She didn't know about the gifts he sent her, her mother probably didn't even know they were from Pop, they were sent through relatives. Elaine would never have dreamed that he kept up with her all through the years. Her pictures were sent to him regularly, but to keep her protected he could not contact her!

Pop called Elaine's dad, Bill Garrett. Bill was the dad who was always there for Elaine. The dad who got Elaine's mother, Dorothy, to take Elaine out of the party dresses and put her into jeans and t-shirts. He changed Elaine from being a "princess" to being a regular kid having fun. Bill loved her, raised her, and will always be her dad.

Elaine said the phone conversation between Bill and Pop went something like this, "Carl called dad and asked his permission to come and see me. Mother was adamantly against it. But dad felt Carl had the right to meet me."

They arranged a time at their home to meet. Pop went to Fairfield and met the family at their house. He and Elaine spent a few hours together. Someone took a picture of Pop and Elaine sitting on the couch together. I know he kept the picture of the two of them along with all he had to remember her by, always.

In January 1967 Pop received a phone call from his brother, Little Earl, telling him that their mother had died. Pop and some of the Shelton family left immediately to go to Fairfield, Illinois, for his mother's funeral.

He was driven to Illinois by one of my cousins. That seemed to be the Shelton tradition – the younger ones driving the uncles around. Pop went to Elaine's home. He knocked on the door. Elaine saw who it was. She followed all the training that she had received from her mother her whole life in that one moment. As she opened the main door she, at the same time, very discreetly, locked the screen door. She said nothing. She just stood there, straight faced, showing no emotion.

"I'm here for my mother's funeral. Can I see you?" was all he said to her.

"I have to call my mother," was Elaine's reply. She left him standing outside the door and went to the phone. Elaine called her mother and told her that Carl was there and wanted to see her. Dorothy said, "Absolutely no!"

Dorothy left work immediately and ran home to Elaine. Her greatest fear was that something would happen to Elaine. Either someone would hurt her in retaliation for the Sheltons, or, and this was her worst fear, that the Sheltons themselves would take Elaine and she would never see her again.

This was a very valid fear. It had already happened once. The youngest of the Sheltons was Pop's Aunt Lula. Lula was the baby of the family and very spoiled. She was a wild child and an even wilder adult. When Lula and her husband James Zuber divorced, James got custody of Jimmy, probably due to Lula's wild, party-girl lifestyle.

James was living in Evansville, Indiana with Jimmy, who was only about four or five years old at the time. James Zuber's dad was the postmaster in Fairfield and James was a mail carrier in Evansville.

Jimmy was playing in the yard at his dad's house when his mom and Big Carl drove up. It was a true child snatching. They grabbed Jimmy, put him in the car and took off. When they got to the New Harmony, Indiana, and were about to cross the river at the state line, they had Jimmy lay down in the back floorboard so he couldn't be seen by police or the toll operators. When they were back on the Illinois side of the line they knew they were home free. Big Carl and Lula didn't visit Evansville after that. There was a warrant out for Lula.

Jimmy didn't see his dad again until he was grown, although his dad sent child support and presents. Jimmy didn't know this. His dad married a woman named Cathy and they moved to the rural area outside Evansville. He continued to work as a mail carrier and raised pigs. They had two daughters. After the girls were grown they contacted Jimmy and they came to Florida to meet. Jimmy took his family to Indiana to meet his dad. James and Cathy visited them in Florida once. Jimmy's wife, Barbara, told me that James kept every issue of the *Wayne County Press*, the local newspaper in Fairfield, where Jimmy was growing up. He probably watched for any news of his son.

I can understand Dorothy being terrified in those brief moments between talking to Elaine on the phone and getting home to see that her daughter was still home and safe. Elaine came back to the door and told Pop that her mother said she could not see him. Pop left. It wasn't until later that Elaine realized Pop said he was there for his mother's funeral, her grandmother! It all happened so fast. Later Elaine had time to think about what had happened and what was said. She had been born and raised in a town of less than 5,000 people and never knew her grandmother was living there!

Of course Elaine asked her mother about her grandmother, "Who was she? Where did she live?"

Her mother's reply was "the Sheltons don't care about anyone but themselves. Why would they care about you?"

The death of her grandmother became a fact that Elaine locked away in the "Shelton box" in her head. Just like I kept knowledge of her locked away in my "Shelton box" in my head. Anything that was put in that "box" didn't have to be thought about or have any emotions attached to it, it just existed.

On the night the Sheltons were leaving Fairfield they went by Dorothy's house. They wanted Elaine and Dorothy to go with them. Elaine was a Shelton and they needed to go with the Sheltons to be protected.

"I have done nothing wrong and I will not leave my home!" Dorothy told them, in no uncertain terms. She stayed in Fairfield and gave Elaine a loving, happy family to grow up in.

It had been more than 16 years since the family originally fled Wayne County. The danger should have been over, but it wasn't until later when I learned more about my grandmother's death did I understand Pop's fear for Elaine.

Pop returned home to Jacksonville after his mother's funeral and there was no continued contact with Elaine with the exception of a letter he sent to her in June 1967. She had already left for college. Bill drove to her college to give her the letter. Elaine didn't reply to it. Pop didn't tell me that he had seen Elaine, and I knew nothing about my grandmother. Maybe the fear of him having gone back to Fairfield and the retaliation it could have brought was the reasoning behind my mother keeping me away from the Sheltons.

After James and I were married in January 1977, we would meet Uncle Earl, Aunt Earline, Pop and whoever was the girlfriend of the day with Pop, for coffee at a local restaurant almost every night. We would have a cup of coffee, maybe a piece of pie and talk, not about anything important, just visiting. When we were ready to leave, Pop, Uncle Earl and James would take turns paying the bill but Uncle Earl would always leave a $20 bill on the table for the tip. The Shelton's were always known for their generosity. After he walked away Aunt Earline would pick up the $20 bill and put it in her purse. She would then lay down a $1 bill in its place.

They lived in a beautiful, two-story brick home here in Jacksonville next to Willowbranch Rose Garden Park. Aunt Earline loved walking through all the beautiful rose bushes. Uncle Earl also owned a place in the country that he called the farm. It was a house he rented out with land where he kept livestock. He loved animals, dogs, horses, cows, goats, I think it's a Shelton trait. Aunt Earline would often get quite upset because Uncle Earl would load up calves or goats he had just bought into the backseat of their very luxurious car to take them to the farm. He never thought a thing about it. The animals were so much more important than any car to him.

The most intriguing story Pop told me had to do with Al Capone, the big-time Chicago gangster. I didn't know anything about the Shelton Gang growing up, but I definitely knew who Alphonse Capone was. Pop said he drove Big Earl from Fairfield, Illinois, to St. Augustine, Florida, to meet with Al Capone. He did this often. Pop was Uncle Earl's driver before he went into the navy in 1942 and after he was discharged.

They met at the Ponce de Leon Hotel. This was a very beautiful and luxurious hotel built by Henry Flagler and opened in 1888. It was very ornately decorated with Tiffany lamps throughout.

Nothing was too extravagant for Henry Flagler! He loved St. Augustine and wanted it to be a place for the rich and famous to visit and vacation. And that's exactly what they did.

Capone and my uncle's meeting was of great interest to me because the hotel is now Flagler College, and I had recently taken my youngest daughter, Krystin, on a fieldtrip to tour the college. The meetings between Big Earl and Capone were to bring and keep peace between the two gangs. They also divided up shipments of liquor at the waterfront. The Shelton's truck would go one way, Capone's car would go the other. Pop said when they were at the hotel, Big Earl and Capone would go in a room for talks and he would wait on them in the lobby. My dad *knew* Al Capone! My uncle was negotiating peace with Al Capone!

But peace wasn't very often the goal of my uncles. Especially when on November 12, 1926, they launched an aerial bombing! Some publications have called this incident, "the first homeland aerial terrorist bombing." I thought this was fascinating! But technically, it wasn't the actual first. The goal of the Shelton attack was to destroy Shady Rest, the hideout of a rival gang headed by Charlie Birger. The chosen aircraft was a "Curtiss Jenny" biplane, a seeming coincidence to me because I named one of my daughters "Jenny." But quite the coincidence when I later found out that Elaine also named one of her daughters "Jenny!" Neither of us knowing each other or anything about the "Curtiss Jenny!"

After Pop was released from the hospital he settled in at home with Nell taking very good care of him. He was so happy to be home and to be spoiled by Nell. We were sitting around talking one day and she told me how she found out about the Shelton Gang. "Pop didn't tell you?" I asked. "No" she said, "your dad never told anyone about his past." One day she picked up a magazine at the local grocery store. When she was reading it later at home she noticed a story about a family with some very familiar names, Big Carl Shelton, Big Earl Shelton, the names of members of Pop's family. Nell asked Pop about the story and he told her that it was his family and he was involved with their activities before and after he was in the navy. He also told her that no one else knew. He emphasized to her that "Ruthie is *not* to know."

Nell was always very loyal to Pop so of course she never told me anything about the Shelton Gang.

It would be several years before I would find out how or when my mother had learned about my dad's past. There are very few people of my parents generation still with us. I went to see one dear, sweet lady who had, many years ago, been a very good friend of my mother. At one time both she and her husband were friendly with my dad, too. I wanted to tell her what I had found out about my dad's past. To my extreme surprise, she already knew about the Shelton Gang!

She told me that my mother had gone to her house one day, long before I was born, with a magazine she wanted kept safe, "in case anything happened to her," were her words to her friend. The magazine had a story in it about the Shelton Gang. My mother knew immediately that this was her husband's family! After that, my dad was no longer welcome in their home. Pop always told me it was because he smoked cigars. After this conversation I knew it was because they didn't want a "gangster" coming around their family. This lady loyally kept my mother's secret until our visit that day just a couple of years ago.

One afternoon I was at Pop's and he was sitting in his big, blue recliner with his cat in his lap, feeding him treats out of his hand, when out of the blue he said, "I used to spend a lot of time in St. Louis, Missouri."

This is how he shared most of his memories with me, all of a sudden he would just start telling me something about his past, I had to always be ready to drop what I was doing and listen.

"Back in my younger days," he went on, "I had friends there."

"That's nice, Pop," I knew there would be more to this story so I sat patiently waiting. I didn't expect what I heard next!

"Their name was Pulitzer. I would spent the night in their house when I was in St. Louis," he thought this was just a matter of fact statement.

I quickly sat on the edge of the couch and looked at him, he just kept petting the cat. "You knew the Pulitzers?!" I could barely get the words out of my mouth, a speechless Shelton – that's something new.

"Nice people," was all he said. I sat there staring at him.

All I could say was, "*The* Pulitzers' of the *St. Louis Post-Dispatch* and Pulitzer Prize fame!"

"Yeah," he was so nonchalant, that was all he had to say.

I think this was certainly a bit of information he could have shared with a teenage daughter who was an aspiring writer! One of the poems I wrote as a young wife and mother had to do with trading in my dream of writing a Pulitzer Prize winning novel for tucking my children into bed every night. And my dad couldn't tell me that he knew this family!

I knew in my head that Pop couldn't have told me this one little fact without opening the floodgates of information that he could *not* share with me. But in my heart I knew that I would never have stopped sending articles into magazines and newspapers for possible publication if I had known that he once had a connection with this family. That knowledge would have been all the encouragement I would ever have needed to keep going.

All those tidbits put together really piqued my curiosity and I told Pop I wanted to know all there was to know about the "Shelton Gang."

Pop told Nell, "get me the book."

"What book?" I said as Nell left the room. "What book?" I was still asking.

"I didn't want anything to do with it when it was being written," Pop explained. "I wouldn't even talk to the author, but now that you know..."

Then it happened – the most confusing and craziest thing that had ever happened to me (up to that point in time) – he handed me the book, *Brothers Notorious: The Sheltons – Southern Illinois' Legendary Gangsters* by Taylor Pensoneau, a book about my family!

"Who *are* you people?" was again all I could think!

Here was a book written and published about my family, the family I never knew existed! A world and a lifetime apart from everything I knew growing up and living my life in Jacksonville.

But this was only the beginning. The next few months turned into years as I searched for any and all information I could find about my newfound family, the "Shelton Gang."

Chapter 3.
Pop Goes Home

I wanted to see where my family was from, the hills Pop played on as a child, the streets he drove down as a teenager, the land where my great-grandparents raised their children. I wanted to see it all through Pop's eyes, hear his stories and see a background behind them. I felt I had so much to catch up on. After a lifetime of knowing nothing about my family I didn't want to waste any time. James said we could go to Fairfield, Illinois, whenever Pop was ready. We had always lived doing things on the spur of the moment, Pop with us, so I thought we would be leaving almost immediately. But that wasn't the way it was with this trip. Pop wouldn't go.

"It's too dangerous for us. They could still be out there," he would say.

The fear and dread he lived with for over 50 years was hard to fight. But I could see in his eyes a longing to go back. He would tell me his stories then sigh and say, "It would be nice to see it all again," then fear would overtake him. I was able to get some pictures of the "old days," as Pop put it, in Fairfield, Illinois. Black and white pictures of the town the way Pop remembered it.

After spending many more hours talking about the past, looking at pictures, reading newspaper articles, Pop consented to go back to his hometown.

"We'll go one day," he said.

"Pop, we need to go now, before it gets too cold." All I could think was what might happen by the next year when it warms up. If we didn't go then, we might not ever get to go together and that was the whole point of the trip – to go with Pop. Then he said the words I'd been hoping to hear, "Let's do it!" Finally, I was going to see where Pop was from. Where my family was from. This was my heritage and I wanted to see everything!

Just two days later in mid-November 2004, we were, as Pop's favorite song says, "on the road again," (Pop loved Willie Nelson). In my favorite picture of Pop and my oldest daughter Missi, he is holding up a handmade sign saying, "On the Road Again."

So here we were, James and I, Krystin, and Pop, all in our Suburban driving across the country. Nell stayed home to take care of their animals so Pop wouldn't worry about them. He had gone on many trips with us over all the years but this would prove to be, by far, the most surprising and eventful of them all. He was so excited about going to Fairfield and showing us around. His stories continued to stream forth. It seemed there was no end to them now. I took in every word he spoke.

We had a very nice trip driving across the country together. We stopped at a roadside park on a lake in Tennessee to enjoy the view while we ate lunch. I made sandwiches and Pop gave Krystin a pocket knife. She whittled away on a stick. It was a very pleasant, relaxing trip.

It was about 9 p.m. when we drove into the edge of town. So this was it, Fairfield, Illinois, the place my family was from. It was a small, quiet town, population about 5,000 the sign said.

"I'll have to check in at the sheriff's office," Pop startled us out of the blue.

I turned and looked at him. He was serious. "What have I gotten us into?" I thought to myself.

"Really?" I asked.

"Really. All Sheltons have to check in at the sheriff's office when they come into town," he answered.

James and I looked at each other, eyes wide open.

"Okay… we'll find the sheriff's office," James said.

It wasn't hard to find in this small town. Find the courthouse and you'll see the jail out back. James parked the Suburban and said he and Krystin would wait on us. As Pop and I walked towards the sheriff's office from the parking lot I remember thinking, "This can't really be happening." When we walked through the doors we found a deputy sitting at the front desk. He looked up as we approached.

"Can I help you?" he asked as Pop reached out his hand.

"Hi, I'm Carl Shelton."

That was the defining moment of this whole experience for me. I thought the deputy was going to fall out of his chair. That was the first time I ever saw the "deer-in-the-headlights look," but it wouldn't be the last. The deputy stood up and they shook hands.

"I don't want any trouble, I'm just here to show my daughter around," Pop continued. "We'll be driving that Suburban around town," he said as he pointed out the door.

They chatted for a minute, the deputy told us where we should stay, and he walked us to the car.

This was my first clue that this Shelton thing was bigger than I had imagined. I was here to see where my family was from, to find the roots I had missed out on knowing about all my life. I wanted to see Pond Creek where my great grandparents raised their family, where my dad tromped around as a kid. I wanted to walk up the hill he and his brother ran up to get the wine they would sneak away to drink. I wanted to find the place where my great Uncle Carl, the man my father was named after, was murdered. But my wishes were soon to take a backseat to what was about to happen when it got around town that "Little Carl" Shelton was back in his hometown.

We stayed at the Briarwood Inn, a nice little hotel at the edge of town. James checked us in and Pop came in so quietly, stealthily, without anyone noticing. It was kind of like a covert operation. Pop waited until there was no one who could see him, then he came past the office. Again, I was standing there, looking at Pop thinking, "who are you?"

The next morning we woke early to a beautiful, cool fall day. I couldn't help but think the weather must have been about the same as the day Uncle Carl was murdered. We talked about all the things we had planned for the day, I wanted to see Pond Creek, Krystin wanted to play, Pop had oil and coal rights that he wanted to transfer to my name. Oh yeah, one more thing I learned about being a Shelton – they were into oil – big oil.

We left the hotel and drove to the town square. When Pop was a teenager Aunt Lula would give him the keys to her car if he would take his younger cousin Jimmy with him to town. As soon as they got there Pop would put Jimmy out on the corner of the square. They were out so late that sometimes Jimmy wondered if he was coming back to get him. But Pop always picked him up and got him home safely. I was loving hearing all these stories! I could never have appreciated it without seeing that quaint little town.

In the middle of the town square was the clock tower. This little town was picture perfect from 1954. I felt as if I had stepped back in time. There were brick streets to walk down. Shops lined the Main Street. As we walked through the town, people were so friendly. They would stop and talk, and this was before they knew who Pop was.

Pop wanted to stop by the *Wayne County Press* to say hi to Tom Matthews, he was the owner of the local newspaper when Pop lived there, not knowing that the paper was now run by his son, Tom Matthews, Jr. We went in and Pop introduced himself to the lady at the front desk and Tom immediately came out. The next thing I knew we were sitting on the couch in Tom's office with him asking Pop questions and typing. Then he had our picture taken. Through it all Pop just kept talking.

"Pop, he's typing everything you say. Pop, maybe you should stop talking," I prodded.

So much for all the caution Pop instilled in me over the last year. Here we were in Fairfield and now everyone would know it. And soon they did!

The paper came out with our family picture on the front page with the caption, "Carl Shelton Returns Home – Last Surviving Member of the Shelton Gang Pays Visit; Reveals Past to His Daughter." Krystin was interested in the actual printing of the newspaper so we were invited to go downstairs and see the print room. Pop, in all his "I'm a star" theme he had going on, pressed his thumb to the ink plate. He, then, held his thumb up to show it, smiled and put his thumbprint on a copy of the newspaper beside his picture. I kept that copy!

We stopped by the *Press* later to pick up a copy of the paper. Word was getting around that "Little Carl" Shelton was at the *Press* office and people were stopping by to meet Pop, to shake his hand, to take a picture with him, even to get his autograph!

This was the most amazing thing I had ever seen, my dad signing autographs for people! We were still in the *Press* office and Pop sat down at a table. He was laughing and talking with everyone.

I heard him say, "This was supposed to be her day," pointing at me, "but I think it turned out to be my day."

People were lining up to get him to autograph their newspapers by his picture. Some even brought in their copy of Pensoneau's book and had Pop sign by his name! Pop kept saying, "Nell's not going to believe this!"

I was having trouble believing it and I was there! Thankfully I had my video camera so we could show Nell that it really happened. Everyone was very nice and respectful. As the article said, Pop was "treated like an aging rock star."

Everyone who came in the newspaper office had a "Shelton story" to tell. These were the good stories, the kind of memories that could be, and should be, passed down to children and grandchildren. People were telling us how the Sheltons helped out their families when times were rough. The good things my family did for other people. It made me feel really good that the family I never knew existed, had touched so many lives with good and people had such fond memories of them.

Then someone brought in and played a copy of the song written in 1948 about the murder of Uncle Carl, "The Death of Carl Shelton." It was written by Fred Henson and Uncle Earl. When it got to the part about Pop's grandmother, Agnes Shelton, Pop broke down and started to cry. Agnes wasn't just a grandmother to Pop, she helped raise him. Although he was enjoying his trip home tremendously, it was also incredibly painful for him. As we were leaving the *Press* office the man asked for Pop's address and told him he would send him a copy of the song. Pop looked at him and said, "I'll give you Ruthie's address."

The man told Pop he understood. Even though Pop was having such a good time, there still was that uneasiness about people knowing where to find him.

We drove out to Pond Creek. Pop showed us what he could from memory. Everything my family had once owned had been bombed or burned to the ground. I tried to imagine what it was like there when Pop was a kid growing up and when my grandfather and great uncles were born and raised there. I don't imagine it would have been very different then.

Pop got to visit a few old friends and make a few new friends. We even had some very nice local people we met join us for supper that night, including Glenda Young, who helped us out at the courthouse, transferring the oil rights. I recently asked her how she felt about meeting my dad, Little Carl.

"It was thrilling," she said, "you could ask him anything, he would tell you."

Also joining us for supper was a volunteer for the Hanna House Museum. She offered to open the museum the next morning for us so we could see the "Shelton Gang" display.

I loved this place we were visiting and no matter how long we would stay on this trip, I knew it wouldn't be long enough and I would come back to it again someday. At that time I had no idea how soon we would be leaving. As we were driving around Fairfield, I noticed a car following us. It wasn't my imagination. We were being followed! I almost walked up to the car when it pulled in across the parking lot where we stopped for gas. I wanted to see who it was and ask them what they wanted, but I didn't.

The day ended at the hotel with us talking about what we were going to do the next day. I especially wanted to spend more time in Pond Creek, we were only there for a few minutes. Pop was starting to express some anxiety about being in Fairfield but I thought it was just because he was tired. I was wrong!

The next morning I went out for coffee and when I returned everyone was up, but the mood had drastically changed from the day before. James opened the door.

"Pop is ready to go home," he told me.

"But we've only been here one day," I said. I couldn't believe that after all this time of not knowing anything about my family and now here we are in their old stomping ground, we had to leave so soon.

"I'm ready to go home," Pop told me. "Too many people know we're here."

It was all becoming too real for Pop and worry was setting in.

I talked him into staying long enough to visit the Hanna House Museum in Fairfield and see the Shelton Gang display. The museum curator was kind enough to offer to open the museum for us that day. She showed us all the exhibits and we were able to read a lot of the newspaper articles about my family. There was an actual display in a museum about my family! This was unbelievable. They were so well-known, infamous I think is the correct word, that there is a museum collection dedicated to them, pictures, newspaper articles, items relating to their gang warfare, even a record of the song, "The Death of Carl Shelton."

This was all becoming a little much for me to handle, too. By noon we were, as Pop put it, "on the road again," heading home to Florida. It was a long, quiet trip home. Our lives would never be the same!

Ruthie Shelton collection

COMING HOME – The author's father, "Little Carl" Shelton, stands with his granddaughter Krystin at the Wayne County Clerk's office in Fairfield during his short trip back to Wayne Co., Illinois.

Chapter 4.
In the Beginning

It was the end of the 19th century in the farmlands of the Midwest. My great grandparents, Benjamin Marsh and Agnes (Gaither) Shelton, were raising their family on a small farm. Ben was born in Kentucky. Agnes was born in Wayne County, Illinois. They both grew up in Wayne County and went to a little log schoolhouse together. They loved each other from the start and married in January 1882. Physically they were both big people, tall and strong, yet opposite in personalities and temperament. Ben was a quiet, calm, and even tempered gentleman. He had already lived through a lot of tragedy in his life.

The Sheltons had migrated from Virginia to Kentucky through several generations of large families. They were fairly wealthy people. The wills of several of my ancestors left to their offspring, houses, livestock, money, land and slaves. My great-great-grandfather Wilson Albert Shelton received a nice sized inheritance from his father. He and his wife Paulina Johnson even bought some of his brothers' inheritances.

They moved to Wayne County, Illinois. Many in the Shelton family had moved there searching for farmland where they could raise their large families. Wilson Albert and Paulina had eight children together, including my great-grandfather Ben. Things were going well for their family until the day tragedy struck. Wilson's wife, the children's mother, Paulina, died. This was a crushing blow to the whole family. They were devastated. Wilson Albert didn't even raise his own children after losing his wife. He farmed them out to relatives to be cared for.

Ben was sent to live with the family of James Raleigh and Tabitha (Young) Shelton elsewhere in Wayne County. James and Ben were first cousins, but James was quite a bit older than Ben. James R. and Tabitha were good people, and they loved Ben dearly. Poor little Ben had lost his mama and now his dad had given him away! Unlike the generations before him, there would be no inheritance for Ben. He would have to work hard for everything he got in life, and that's what he did. The last that was known of Ben's father, Wilson Albert, was related by one of Wilson Albert's grandsons who said, "Wilson remarried and she broke him."

Agnes was kind of rough around the edges, had her opinions and gave them, and she never cared what other people thought. She was quick with her words and quick with her temper. When she was riled up, Ben would just go outside and wait for her to cool down. But she also was a very giving person. She was known for feeding the homeless people that would come around. And they all seemed to know where to go for food. Sometimes she made them work first but they didn't mind. They knew a good, hot meal awaited them at the end of the day.

For all their differences Ben and Agnes had two things in common, they loved each other and they loved their family. Every time Ben walked through the kitchen and Agnes was standing at the stove cooking, he would pop her on the bottom. They both loved their family very much. For Ben, sometimes this meant a sort of tough love towards his boys. After the Shelton boys grew up and became the notorious Shelton Gang, he withdrew further from them. By the end of his life he would not even discuss his sons with the curious and the onlookers.

In all their years together my great grandparents never wavered in who they were. They stayed true to their beliefs and their moral values. For Ben it was his great sense of what was right. He did not condone the way his sons, Carl, Earl and Bernie lived their lives and he let it be known.

Agnes was, of course, another story. From the beginning to the end of her long life of raising her family, in her eyes, her children could do no wrong. She always saw the good in her boys, and only the good. The words, "not my boys," came out of her mouth many times over the years. She never looked back to see if she could ever have been wrong about her boys. She focused straight ahead, unyielding in her loyalty to her family, willing to do anything and everything in her power to help them, legal or not.

There were five Shelton boys. They were Roy, born in 1885; Carl, born in 1888; Earl, born in 1890; Dalta (my grandfather), born in 1893; and Bernie, born in 1899. There were three daughters. Nora was the first child born to Ben and Agnes Shelton in 1883. The first tragedy of Agnes' long and eventful life proved to be when her eldest daughter died at the age of 13. Little Nora was buried in West Cemetery, in Wayne County, Illinois. Only two daughters lived to adulthood, Hazel, born 1904, and Lula, the always spoiled baby girl of the family, born in 1909.

The five boys were into trouble from the time they could run around Pond Creek on their own. They were always fighting with other kids. They were known as bullies and thieves. They were big from genetics and strong from working on the farm. Though they tried to do as little work as possible. As the boys got big, very big, people were becoming more and more afraid of them. The neighbors just tried to stay out of their way.

They would steal anything they wanted, a horse blanket, a harness, even a bucket of corn, if the Shelton boys wanted something they just walked away with it. If anyone dared to cross them, the boys would retaliate, sometimes in very violent ways.

This was in spite of the fact that Ben tried to raise all his children to be good god fearing people. He had his whole family attend the Methodist Church in Merriam. Agnes sang in the choir. Ben was the church leader for quite a few years and always had an active role in the congregation. Ben even made Uncle Carl play the piano and teach a Sunday school class. But it didn't change him or his brothers. Uncle Carl hated being made to do anything, although he did enjoy playing the piano and he did so the rest of his life.

Uncle Carl especially hated school. He was once threatened by a teacher that if he continued to be late for school he was going to whip him. In his article, "The Sheltons: America's Bloodiest Gang," published by the *Saturday Evening Post* in 1950, John Bartlow Martin reported that Uncle Carl's reply to his teacher's threat was, "All right, you'll have to whip me every morning then, and I'll whip you when I'm grown." Uncle Carl didn't get whipped by that teacher.

There was another member of the family that had quite an influence on my uncles as they were growing up, but not in a good way. It was Ben's brother, Albert H. Shelton, called "Ab" by his family.

"He was the black sheep of the family," I was told. That was a big statement, considering what family we are talking about. Ab was a professional riverboat gambler. He showed the Shelton boys a totally different lifestyle than the one their father offered them. It was a lifestyle that seemed to be filled with glitz and glamour. It really shined to my uncles. You could turn a quick buck, lift nothing more than a finger in a day's work and be surrounded by liquor and fast women all the time. They just didn't see the downside of Ab's life. Ben was nothing like him and this probably drew his boys to associate even more with their Uncle Ab.

I was contacted by one of Ab's great-granddaughters. She told me, "Ab was a riverboat gambler. He misled the Shelton boys literally into a life of crime. He led them into destroying themselves."

Ab lived in Wayne County as well. He had three children. Two sons, one that he didn't claim, and a daughter, Leona "Lee" that was too much like him for her own good. His daughter was very close to all the Shelton boys.

"They took care of her, helped her. Came to pick her up in cars shot full of holes and her children were out in the yard sticking their fingers in the bullet holes," her great-granddaughter continued.

Apparently the Shelton boys loved this cousin so much that they paid all the bills for her surgery when she had cancer. I asked the great-granddaughter to tell me more about Ab.

"He just couldn't play a straight deck. Everything he touched turned into something bad. He changed later but only after he lost everything he loved," she said.

Ab died in 1962 at the age of 97 and is buried in Wayne County.

Big Carl married Lula Woods January 10, 1909. He was just 21 years old when they married. At 24 years old he was a widower. He lost his beloved Lula to influenza. She was only 23 years old when she died. A relative of his deceased wife told me that Uncle Carl kept her ring the rest of his life, she was that precious to him.

Carl went to St. Louis, Missouri and did some work there. For a while he drove cabs. This was probably the first job he ever did that he had a real knack for. Driving cars fast and wild seems to be in the Shelton blood.

Photograph courtesy of Jimmy Zuber

FUN TIME – Bernie Shelton takes his little sister Lula out on a lake or pond probably near the family farm in Wayne County sometime in the mid to late 1910s.

Roy spent some time in St. Louis with Big Carl driving cabs. He married Stella Lela Renfro in 1905. They had two sons, Wesley Aaron, born on May 4, 1906, and Willard in 1909. But having sons was not enough to keep Roy out of trouble. Roy loved cars, especially other peoples' cars. He was arrested and spent a lot of time in jail for car stealing among other crimes. His wife took the boys and moved to Chicago to live with relatives. By April 1910 he had divorced and went to live with Carl and Lula in University City, Missouri, a suburb just across the line on the west side of St. Louis. Both he and Carl worked as motormen on the streetcars.[1]

In my research I found out that Stella had later moved to Florida like the rest of the Shelton clan. She died in New Port Richey in 1975 at the age of 89. Wesley married and had one daughter. I was thrilled to talk with her and hear that Roy's children led very happy, well-adjusted lives.

Some years ago after being contacted by Aunt Hazel about some Shelton oil rights, Wesley learned where his father's family was. He took his family to visit Big Earl in Jacksonville. On seeing his nephew, Uncle Earl's eyes filled with tears. Wesley looked so much like Earl's brother Roy. Wesley died on November 3, 1982, in New Port Richey too, seven years after his mother. His brother Willard married and led a very active life filled with a lot of excitement and travel. He had no children but lived to be about 95 years old. He died in Florida in 2004.

Uncle Earl had left home by 1910, but I haven't found where he went. The younger children including my grandfather Dalta, Bernie

---

[1] 1910 Census of St. Louis Co., Missouri. Ancestry.com.

and the girls remained at home with Ben and Agnes in Wayne County.[2]

Roy couldn't stay with his younger brother for long. Within a few years he moved across the river to Madison, just south of Granite City in Madison County. On November 28, 1912, he married again to Minnie Butler in Clayton, Missouri, the county seat of St. Louis County.[3]

Dalta, my grandfather, married Mamie Conaway in 1912. They buried a baby daughter near her parents, John and Emma Conaway, in Ebenezer Cemetery in Wayne County. In 1914 Dalta married my grandmother, Lillie Myers Biggs. That was a marriage doomed from the start. Dalta was never one to settle down, no matter what a piece of paper said. Lillie had a son from her first marriage, Edward Biggs, then she and Dalta had three children together.

Big Earl married Edith Gurley in 1913. She was a local girl and they spent their time together on the farm. But their time together was very limited. They weren't compatible. Maybe she sensed the life he had before him. Soon the marriage ended. By the end of the decade she had moved to Anderson, Indiana, and worked as an assembler. She got sick though and returned home to her parents where she died on November 7, 1920, at the age of 26.[4]

Uncle Earl took the divorce very hard. He found himself hanging out at the Fairfield town square and the local pool hall with no point to his life. With nothing better to do with his time than shoot pool or

---

[2] 1910 Census of Wayne Co., Missouri. Ancestry.com.

[3] Missouri Marriage Records, 1805-2002. Ancestry.com.

[4] 1920 Census of Madison Co., Indiana. Ancestry.com; Illinois, Deaths and Stillbirths Index, 1916-1947. Ancestry.com; and "Edith Alice Gurley Shelton." FindaGrave.com.

play cards for money, you could bet he was headed for trouble. And he found it.

It was in March 1915 that he had his first real experience with police, courts and jail, and about the only time my uncles couldn't buy their way out of trouble. Earl was still living in Pond Creek and he had a neighbor Cloyd Wilson who shared a ride in his horse and buggy from time to time home from Fairfield. The way the story goes is that they had been playing cards together and Earl caught Wilson cheating! Earl saw it that he was just taking back what was his. One thing I was taught young – you don't cheat at cards and if you do cheat – you *don't* get caught!

Earl later borrowed five dollars from Wilson himself and bought a gun with it. Wilson had no idea that Earl knew he had cheated at cards or that his entire life was about to turn upside down because of it. Uncle Earl gave the gun to a man named Thomas Draper and told him to rob Wilson. It still amazes me that my uncles could have any one do whatever they wanted just by a word.

Earl was again riding home from Fairfield with Wilson in Wilson's buggy, as if nothing had happened, when Draper jumped out from a bridge onto the road and grabbed the horse to stop the buggy. He said for them to get down, it was a hold-up. Earl got down and went straight over to Draper and stood by him! Wilson thought they were joking until he saw the gun. Then he knew it was for real. Draper took Wilson's money, gold watch and ring, then he told Wilson and Earl they could go.

Draper was arrested the next day because he fit the description of the robber given to police by Wilson. Earl, of course, denied that it was Draper who robbed Wilson, but Draper had not been smart enough to dispose of the gun Earl had given him and this led to my uncle being tied in with the crime. The man who sold Earl the gun for five dollars identified it as the one he sold to Earl the night before. Earl and Draper were both arrested on charges of robbery and conspiracy.

This is when true Shelton colors started to show. Earl tried to bribe Wilson with $500 to get him to drop the charges, Wilson refused. Then Earl bribed certain politicians to have his case tried separately from Draper's case.

That's when Carl got in the picture. He came back to Fairfield from St. Louis and repeatedly threatened Wilson. Wilson still didn't give in. When offers of money and threats of violence didn't make Wilson back down, Carl brought in a couple of thugs from St. Louis to take care of Wilson, but Wilson had a cousin in St. Louis, Frank Crews, who was able to warn him. Crews' wife had overheard the Sheltons planning the assault on Wilson and immediately told her husband about it. Crews let his cousin know what was being planned and Wilson stayed out of harm's way.

Now the Sheltons had a vendetta against Crews and his wife. They threatened Crews' wife if she didn't leave town. Crews went to the St. Louis police and told them about the threat against his wife. He also told them that Carl had stolen a car the year before in St. Louis. The police charged Earl with compounding a felony. Carl was charged with compounding a felony *and* grand larceny! They arrested Carl on June 12, 1915. Later his FBI rap sheet would simply list the charge as "gangster."[5]

Thomas Draper's case was much simpler than Big Earl's case. Draper was sentenced in Fairfield in June.

---

[5] Carl Shelton (#27024) Inmate File. Leavenworth Penitentiary Records. National Archives-Kansas City. Dec. 13, 1935. Federal Bureau of Investigation Form G (rap sheet).

The Sheltons offered a man in St. Louis a horse and wagon if he would lie to the police and say that Crews had stolen a ring from him. The man went to the police with his accusation and they went out to arrest Crews.

By now Crews was such a nervous wreck from all the threats against him and his wife, that he shot the officers thinking they were the Sheltons coming to kill them. One officer lost a finger and Crews was shot in the lung during the gun play. Crews was arrested but later released when the man confessed that it was all a set up instigated by my uncles.

Agnes showed her loyalty to her boys and proved that she really would do anything for them, legal or not. She went to the sheriff in Fairfield acting the part of a terrified victim. She told the sheriff that Wilson's mother had attacked her. These women were neighbors and Agnes accused her of an attack with a butcher knife. Agnes was not believed. Wilson was sure that the Sheltons were going to get off free. He was not a rich man yet he spent his own money to hire the best lawyers Fairfield had to offer to assist the state's attorney with the case. He was determined to get justice.

By the end of it all, both of my uncles were sent to jail. Uncle Earl was sentenced to the state reformatory at Pontiac in October 1915, and 18 months later he was paroled. Uncle Carl earned a year in the workhouse in St. Louis.

Cloyd Wilson and my uncles had known each other for years, grown up together, went to school together, now their friendships and their parents' friendships were ruined. The case cost Wilson a whole summer's work and $1,000 out of his pocket. I wonder if he and Uncle Earl thought it was all worth it.

In 1917 Earl was out of jail and together with Carl in St. Louis again. Bernie was spending as much time as he could with them, even though he was still just a teenager. The older he got the less he got along with his dad Ben and the more trouble he got into. He was arrested in St. Louis in a stolen car, but not surprisingly, he didn't serve any prison time for it. By 1918, all five brothers lived in St. Louis, three were chauffeurs and two worked for the St. Louis Dairy Co.

When Carl registered for the draft on June 5, 1917, he was single again and had moved into the city on the south side. If the big city opened the Shelton boys' eyes to the larger world – and St. Louis was big then, the fourth largest city in the country in 1910, and though it was still growing, the 6th largest in 1920 – it had to be Carl's new job that showed him just what money could buy.

By the time of the draft he worked as a chauffeur for John L. Green, president of the Laclede-Christy Clay Products Company of St. Louis who lived in a palatial estate at 12 Kingsbury Place in the ritzy Central West End. Green employed a thousand men at his two plants and two live-in servants in his household. For the first time Carl found himself among people at the pinnacle of society, even if he was just holding open the car door for them. He was 29 and single, no wife, no kids and no future.[6]

Carl shared his place with his brother Earl who also registered that day. Earl worked for the St. Louis Dairy Co. at 2008 Pine Street as a dairy laborer. That's close to being a bottler and he probably picked up some skills that came to good use during Prohibition. He was described as six feet tall with a stout build. More than his

---

[6] World War I Draft Registration Cards, 1917-1918. Ancestry.com; and Illinois Statewide Death Index, 1916-1950. Illinois State Archives. The draft card lists his address as 3345 Morgan which is probably Morgan Ford Road. For more on his employer John L. Green see Dec. 17, 1918. "In the Wake of the News." *Brick and Clay Record*. Chicago: Kenfield-Leach Co. 53:13. 1077; and 1920 Census of St. Louis, Mo. Ancestry.com.

brothers he must have been the one left to support the family. He listed his parents and two sisters as dependent on him.

Whatever skills he didn't pick up as a laborer his brother Dalta might have picked up in the lab there. He lived at 2027 Franklin Avenue with my grandmother Lillie, and their two children, her son and their daughter.

On September 12, 1918, another round of draft registrations took place, including Roy who was still living with Minnie but had moved back to St. Louis. He worked as a chauffeur like Carl, except he didn't have an employer at the time. They lived at 2110 Washington Avenue. Bernie lived above them at 2110½ Washington. He followed the family tradition and worked as a chauffeur as well for a firm called Hill & King at 3708 Page Avenue.[7]

The St. Louis police were soon growing tired of the antics of the Shelton boys and suggested that they leave St. Louis, which they did looking for greener pastures. They thought this might be in the coal mining towns of Southern Illinois.

Before he moved Carl found another wife, Marguerite Bender, a divorcee who had filed for divorce from her husband in August of 1917. The court granted the divorce in December 1919 and by January 10, 1920, Carl, Marguerite and his new eight-year-old stepdaughter Alice lived at 903 Willow Street in Carterville. Carl was listed as working as a pumpman at a coal mine.[8] The marriage also brought two stepsons as well, at least one of whom would end up in the gang by the end of the decade.

Roy lived just up the road with a new wife at 514 Nevada St., and still worked as a chauffeur for a service car. Earl rounded out the

---

[7] World War I Draft Registration Cards, 1917-1918. Ancestry.com.

[8] 1920 Census of Williamson Co., Illinois. Ancestry.com.

Sheltons in Carterville at that point. He worked as a coal miner and boarded at Achsah Norton's hotel downtown. Bernie and my grandfather Dalta haven't been found in the census that year while Ben and Agnes still had the two girls with them up in Wayne County.[9] They wouldn't be there long. Within two or three years everyone ended up in Bloody Williamson where my dad, Little Carl, would be born in 1924.

During this time they were making acquaintances that would later be very useful to their business endeavors as well as criminal enterprises. Roy would be the first to get caught. On October 15, 1921, a Williamson County jury found him guilty of burglary and larceny after stealing a car off of the courthouse square in Marion, the county seat of Williamson County. At the time he claimed to have been working as a farmhand.

The year of 1922 would become a turning point for both the Shelton family as well as Williamson County. The year started out with Carl, Earl and Bernie all working in the local coal mines. In March Carl made the news in neighboring Carbondale, and amazingly it had nothing to do with stolen cars, booze, guns or anything else that would soon be associated with his name. Instead, it was about a race. On March 9, he made a bet that he could run from Carterville to Carbondale, about 10 miles away, and back in under four hours – and in the rain!

"Shelton was an athlete in school and is wearing a track suit on his run. The judges with him are in cars," the Carbondale paper noted. He left Carterville at 1:45 p.m. and arrived in Carbondale at

---

[9] 1920 Census of Williamson Co., Illinois; and 1920 Census of Wayne Co., Illinois. Ancestry.com.

3:30 p.m. He was to run down the railroad track for the return trip. The paper didn't mention whether he made it in time.[10]

The levity would soon end though. The United Mine Workers of America began a nationwide strike on April 1. Roy, apparently spent the first part of the year in the county jail, not arriving at the Southern Illinois Penitentiary at Menard until April 23, to begin a sentence of one to 20 years.[11]

With Roy out of the picture and Dalta seemingly assigned to look out for the parents, as far as the world would know the Shelton Brothers would just be Carl, Earl and Bernie.

Photo courtesy of Jimmy Zuber

ON THE FARM – Ben and Agnes at home with the chickens, most likely on their Wayne County farm.

---

[10] March 9, 1922. "Man Running From Here to C'Ville on Wager in 4 Hours." *The Free Press* (Carbondale, Ill.). 1.

[11] Taylor Pensoneau. 2002. *Brothers Notorious*. New Berlin, Ill.: Downstate Publications. 18; Aug. 4, 1927. "Roy Shelton Returned to Menard Penitentiary." *The Daily Independent* (Murphysboro, Ill.). 1; and April 23, 1922. "Williamson County." County Intake Registers. Menard Correctional Center. Illinois State Archives.

Photo courtesy of Jimmy Zuber

SHELTONS IN CARTERVILLE – Roy and Dalta Shelton are missing in this photo, but the better known brothers, their sisters and parents were present. From the left standing, Hazel, Carl, Earl, Lula and Bernie. Sitting are Agnes and Ben.

Chapter 5.

Early Days in the Gang

During the morning of June 22, 1922, hundreds of striking UMWA coal miners led 40 or so replacement workers and guards away from the Lester strip mine between Marion and Herrin.

Within a matter of hours, about half of the men would be dead, massacred in the woods, chased across area farms, or had their throats slit in the city cemetery. Immediately this became known across the country as the Herrin Massacre.

The Shelton Brothers may have been there participating. Their saving grace it would seem, was that they were already involved in a crime spree across a number of Southern states that spring and summer. They had probably left Carterville after the sheriff took Roy off to the pen. Uncle Carl's FBI record showed him arrested in San Antonio, Texas, the day before the massacre using the alias of Harry Henderson Hill. They charged him with vagrancy, a charge often brought against gangsters who couldn't show evidence of a job. It was harassment, but the goal wasn't jail. For the law, it was just to get them out of their town.

Fifty days after the massacre police in Little Rock, Arkansas, arrested Carl, Earl and Bernie along with a fourth man.[12] They told police they were simply "peaceful Herrin miners."[13]

---

[12] Carl Shelton (#27024) Inmate File. Leavenworth Penitentiary Records. National Archives-Kansas City. Dec. 13, 1935. Federal Bureau of Investigation Form G (rap sheet).

Police arrested them after following a tip to the police chief about the presence of "four Chicago gun men (who) were in the city."

"Whether or not they really are gunmen remains to be seen," one of the papers noted the next day, "but they might easily have been such judging from the fact that two of them were armed with revolvers, an automatic pistol, a sawed off shot gun, (and) a pair of bolt cutters. A large quantity of ammunition for both the shot gun and the small arms were found in the automobile."

My uncles denied they had been in Herrin the day of the massacre, only admitting they had been in Little Rock for about 10 days. The police tip noted they "had a habit of remaining under cover during the day and going out in their machine at night. When asked about the weapons they just answered, "we just happened to have them."

In their belongings police found no real identification, but did find a button, "such as is worn by rescue workers of the Illinois mines." Receipts and other papers told the detectives, "the men had been in Mississippi, Alabama, Missouri, Illinois, Arkansas and several other states."

They also had addresses of men they were to meet later in the month in St. Louis, Missouri, and Rochester, New York. They told police they were simply on their way to Hot Springs, Arkansas. The latter two towns were known for their gambling resorts. What had made police nervous were reports that every night the men would be found on Main Street, but had always parked on Scott Street.

---

[13] Oldham Paisley, comp. 2006. *Newspaper Articles from Oldham Paisley's Scrapbooks, Volume 5-6, Klan-Young-Birger.* Marion, Ill.: Williamson County Historical Society. 67. Specifically, Nov. 4, 1926. "Shelton Boys Too Reckless For Me, Brother Asserts." *St. Louis Star* (St. Louis, Mo.).

Within a day of investigation police determined the Sheltons had been part of a larger group that held up two Little Rock men riding home from their work at the railroad shops.

The two "were in a Ford touring car, driven by a negro. As they neared a bridge on the Frazier pike, a touring car stopped across their path and from it alighted seven men, who said they were officers and pretended to believe that (the pair) were bootleggers. The car with the two men and their captives was driven to a grove near Picron, where all got out."

One of the men robbed the first victim of $60 and "struck him with his fist" when the man told him he had nothing more in his pockets. The victim then managed to get away and ran back to Little Rock where he reported the crime to police. The seven then let the other man eventually go as well.

During questioning Bernie admitted to being photographed by St. Louis police before, but "operated a jitney in the Illinois coal mine district until labor trouble developed." Earl said he owned a taxicab in St. Louis, Mo., while Carl said he had been out of work since the strike began in April. He said he had worked in the Herrin mines for five years, "until the strike, and since then has been traveling over the country." Five years put him back to 1917 when he was a chauffeur in St. Louis, but it also matches another account that he had worked at least briefly at a mine in neighboring Franklin County prior to World War I. For someone out of state that would still be considered a Herrin-area mine.

The court system didn't buy their stories of innocence. On the stand Carl said he had made $249 a month prior to the strike and that he and his brothers were in St. Louis the day of the massacre. A deputy marshal who may have been the one that tipped off police in the first place said he saw the men at the Missouri Pacific railroad station two or three nights prior to their arrest and that two of them had followed him and his wife into the station. He said his wife had seen the men drive past their home on several occasions.

Carl claimed they were just visiting the station at noon and 8 p.m. each night to see if a friend was a passenger on the trains arriving in Little Rock. A blackjack found in the car, he said, belonged to his father who was a night watchman at Herrin. He "supposed the parent left it in the automobile."

As to the two highway robbery victims, they claimed they couldn't positively identify the men. Maybe that was true. Maybe it had something to do with the other three robbers still at large.

A judge gave Carl, Earl, and the fourth man, William E. Todd, each a three-month term at the county farm and a $100 fine. Bernie, who had been unarmed at the time of the arrest got off once again. All in all they were fortunate. The detective working their case was shot to death the following night responding to another crime scene in the railroad yards. Had he been around to continue his investigation who knows what he might have discovered.[14] Bernie's ability to escape responsibility continued as he returned to Southern Illinois to face an auto theft charge in Jackson County. On September 15, a jury took 19 minutes to find him not guilty again.[15]

When Carl and Earl finally got back home later that year the Herrin Massacre trials had everyone's attention. There were two

---

[14] Aug. 12, 1922. "Police Holding Three Herrin, Ill., Miners." *Arkansas Democrat* (Little Rock, Ark.). 3; Aug. 12, 1922. "Herrin, Ill., Men In Custody Here." *The Arkansas Gazette* (Little Rock, Ark.). 1; Aug. 13, 1922 "Herrin Men Are Robbery Suspects." *The Arkansas Gazette* (Little Rock, Ark.). 1; Aug. 18, 1922. "Illinois Gunmen To State Farm." *The Arkansas Gazette* (Little Rock, Ill.). 5; and Aug. 17, 1922. "Two Illinois Miners Are Given Heavy Sentences." *Arkansas Democrat* (Little Rock, Ark.) 1.

[15] Sept. 16, 1922. "Boy Charivari Slayer Held on Murder Charge." *The Free Press* (Carbondale, Ill.). 1

trials, one starting in November and the second in early 1923. In both cases the jurors would find all of the defendants not guilty. Beginning that January a series of public meetings started encouraging a tougher take on law and order. Part of it was to secure a jury that would convict the miners involved in the massacre, but it was also a reaction to the growing bootlegging and crime in the county.[16]

My uncles may not have had anything to do with the former, but they definitely had something to do with the latter. By the end of October 1923, Bernie and Charley Biggs (most likely the Charlie Briggs who would play a growing role in the gang in the following year) sat in the Williamson County Jail for "terrorizing autoists on the west hard road for some times. Parties from Carbondale were expected Saturday afternoon to identify them in connection with another hold up."[17]

Earl, on the other hand, had hooked up with Jack Skelcher, and opened a roadhouse that fall in Colp, a rough mining community of around 2,000 north of Carterville and west of Herrin that had the nickname of "Pistol City."

"Business was good that fall," a later business manager for the gang wrote, "The Williamson County mines were all working and money was plentiful. The dice table and booze business at the Shelton place were showing good profits and everything was jake."[18]

Skelcher along with Briggs would become the two most trusted henchmen in the early days of the gang. Skelcher's brother Dwight

---

[16] George Galligan and Jack Wilkinson. 1927, Reprinted 1985. *In Bloody Williamson*. Marion, Ill.: Williamson County Historical Society. 24.

[17] Oct. 27, 1923. "Believed to Have Right Robbers." *Marion Evening Post* (Marion, Ill.). 1.

[18] Ralph Johnson and Jon Musgrave. 2010. *Secrets of the Herrin Gangs*. Marion, Ill.: IllinoisHistory.com. 8.

had already been arrested earlier that year for robbing a bank in Franklin County.[19]

Uncle Carl was moving up in the ranks in the mining field and eventually moved to Herrin, Illinois to work. But working in the coal mines was not the life my uncles wanted. The work was hard and the pay was never enough to support the lifestyle they wanted.

So again they moved on. The only stability in their lives was that little farm house where they would visit their parents, Agnes and Ben. Uncle Carl was a true mama's boy. All through his life when he was in Pond Creek to take care of farming business, he always made time to stop by his childhood home to see his mama and enjoy a good home cooked meal. They would sit in the same kitchen where he grew up, Agnes' homemade pies cooling in the window, and they would talk, laugh, even cry.

By the early 1920s Carl and Earl made their way to East St. Louis, Illinois. This was a time and place that law enforcement seemed to forget. A town where the gangsters ran the streets openly and freely and the ladies of the night provided the entertainment day and night with no regard to laws or morals. It was a city that the Shelton boys found ripe for the taking and take it they did!

Carl and Earl opened a saloon at 19th and Market Avenue and took rooms at the Arlington Hotel on Missouri Avenue. This was a pivotal turning point in the Shelton boys' lives. From here on out they would no longer be considered just neighborhood thugs or small town bullies. The Shelton boys from Pond Creek were about to become and be known to all as the "Shelton Gang!"

---

[19] Oct. 5, 1922. "Two Suspected Bank Robbers Under Arrest." *Benton Republican* (Benton, Ill.). 1

Chapter 6.
Growing in Power

In East St. Louis, Illinois, the Arlington Hotel was owned by Art Newman. Born in southeastern Tennessee, he came to Illinois with his family in the 1910s to work the region's coal mines, but like the Sheltons he longed for something easier than mining. He went to work as a salesman for the Royal Tea Company out of Springfield and found life on the road a great opportunity for other projects. Soon he moved to East St. Louis. There he married a widow and formidable woman in her own right named Bessie.[20] Together they developed their own life of crime. Not surprisingly, he and the Shelton boys quickly became friends. They felt they had the same interests in business and in criminal activities.

Art Newman's wife Bessie had a different opinion of Earl, Carl, and Bernie. She hated them! She ran one of the most popular and best money making brothels in East St. Louis, right there in the Arlington Hotel. She felt the Shelton boys scared away her girls' customers. The boys were very cocky, sporting their nice clothes and big diamonds, cleaning their guns in the lobby. They were always aiming their guns at people, just for fun. When hothead Bernie would visit them, he would start a fight with anyone if they just looked at him wrong. And Bernie made sure a lot of people "looked

---

[20] 1900 Census of Hamilton Co., Tennessee, 1910 Census of Franklin Co., Arkansas, and 1920 Census of St. Clair Co., Illinois. Ancestry.com; and U.S. World War I Draft Registration Cards, 1917-1918. Ancestry.com.

at him wrong." It seemed he just lived for a fight. He didn't care who or where it was, he was always ready for a brawl.

This was a place that offered nothing but the worst in associations. The Shelton boys were meeting people who would hold the cards in their later lives, particularly the Ace of Spades! One of these associates was Freddie Wooten, a friend of Art Newman. Others they met would later side with or against them. This was quite a turning point in their lives.

With their liquor business flourishing, my uncles decided to expand their saloons into Southern Illinois. Pop told me that Big Earl and Big Carl told my grandfather, Dalta, "stay home and take care of the folks, we'll send money." He was said to be "too hotheaded and not smart enough" to be part of the gang. Though he was deemed "not smart enough" to be *in* the gang, he did later work for his brothers and he was the one "smart enough" to survive the later assassinations and attempted assassinations of most of his family!

Pop and the other relatives who told me more about my grandfather, often illustrated the "not smart enough comment" with the following story. One night Dalta was dealing cards at the Sheltons' gambling place downtown Fairfield. A man had lost all his money at the table and asked Dalta to front him five dollars. Dalta told him he needed a hubcap for his car, if he got one, he'd give him the money. The man left and was gone a while. When he came back he handed a hubcap to Dalta. It matched the one missing so my grandfather gave him the five dollars and the man went back to gambling. When Dalta left work he walked down to his car. Instead of missing one hubcap he was now short two.

With Prohibition becoming the law of the land in January 1920, the brothers, and particularly Earl, developed the ability to not only get the liquor from the Bahamas but to run it undetected all the way into the Midwest. Finally, the Shelton boys were stepping into the gold mine they had always wanted. If anyone in the area wanted to sell booze they had to buy it, and they had to buy it from the Shelton boys!

Earl knew where the liquor was and how to bring it into the states for distribution. Before the 18th Amendment there had been a patchwork of local prohibition laws, and then finally a nation-wide temporary prohibition during World War I. Now, for those who knew and were daring, there was big money to be made.

There were four main areas in the United States that become the route to bring in the now illegal liquor. On land it was carried in through Chicago and Detroit by trucks and cars outfitted to hold every case, bottle and gallon that could possibly be squeezed in undetected. But by sea it was brought onto U.S. soil by way of New York in the north and Florida in the south by boat. The origin of the liquor was the Bahamas, just 60 miles offshore from West Palm Beach, Florida. The boat captains were willing to take the risk of arrest and the impoundment of their boats for the high pay they received as they hauled in cases of liquor. Like the cars and trucks that ran the contraband across the nation, these boats had souped up engines, sometimes powered by army surplus Liberty airplane engines. The U.S. Coast Guard could only try to catch these high powered, wave jumping vessels. But they were sorely out powered. They would seemingly fly across the ocean leaving the U.S. Coast Guard ships in their wake.

Big Earl would meet the boats that brought the liquor in from the Bahamas. Sometimes he took a launch out to meet the boats that brought it in. He would board the boat with the haul while it was still offshore. They would dock at Ponce Inlet, St. Johns County,

Florida, about 12 miles south of Daytona Beach, Florida. At the time the area was known as Mosquito Inlet.

What began in 1887 as Mosquito Inlet Lighthouse, is now known as Ponce de Leon Inlet Light Station. It is the tallest lighthouse in Florida, the second tallest on the east coast of the United States. You can climb the 203 steps to the top for the most breathtaking views. Before I found out anything about the Shelton Gang, my youngest daughter Krystin and I climbed that lighthouse. We stood at the top for a few minutes admiring that incredible view, then we came back down the 203 steps, looked at each other and said, "Yeah, let's go again," and we went back up. I find it so amazing that a story about the family I never knew I had in the Midwest kept crossing my path in Florida so many years later!

Big Earl and his men would meet the boat. He had to have several men working for him to take care of business fast and efficiently. They would load the liquor from the boat into cars and trucks with drivers waiting in each. The Shelton boys had men on their payroll whose job it was to reconstruct these outwardly normal looking vehicles to carry as much contraband as possible. There were hidden compartments built under and behind the seats and under the floorboards. Each car could carry as much as 400 quart bottles.

Trucks also were rigged to haul booze in specially-designed hidden compartments in the back, anyone inspecting them would think they were empty. The largest transport the Sheltons used to haul the booze was a "gasoline truck." At least that's what it looked like. It could carry 110 gallons of actual gas. This came in handy for the liquor runners when they needed to be refueled during their flight to the Midwest. The gas was contained in the back of the tank and there was an outside faucet so that a hose could be attached and the gas could be pumped into another car. But in reality it was a liquor hauler in disguise. Behind the driver's seat there was a concealed opening that led to the main tank. The main tank carried the real cargo, up to 80 cases of whiskey.

The liquor runners then headed north towards Jacksonville, Florida. In the beginning they diverted around Jacksonville and other big cities but once they started driving cars and trucks with souped up engines, they ran straight through. The Shelton boys also had mechanics on the payroll whose job it was to make their cars faster and lighter than anything else on the road. Nothing and no one could catch them!

About this time the Earl and Carl met up again with Charlie Birger. Born of Russian immigrant parents, Birger was a small man with a very large ego and an almost insatiable desire for riches and respect, though he never earned much of either. He was a criminal, a gambler, and had his own "gang" established after leaving the coal mines. Having the liquor distribution business in common, Birger was an early customer of the Shelton boys. He bought liquor from them he then resold. But people didn't get what they thought they were paying for. Birger was wily and deceitful, even with his own customers. Before he redistributed the liquor, Birger always cut it. What he sold was only one-fifth as strong as it was when it started.

Soon Birger and Carl aligned themselves together and used what talents each of them had to totally take over the gambling and liquor markets in Southern Illinois. Carl could smooth talk anyone to get what they wanted, and if that didn't work, Bernie would be more than happy to rough them up. Big Carl and Birger had both learned to slick the palms of any law enforcement individuals that might get in the way of the liquor and gambling establishments they were setting up.

In East St. Louis Newman's wife had grown so tired of the antics of Carl and Bernie at the Arlington Hotel that she made Art order all the Sheltons to move out. For a while they went to the nearby Savoy Hotel to stay while their business was growing and expanding. Soon they were living in very nice houses in the most well to do neighborhoods. They were driving the best cars and wearing expensive clothes and jewelry, Bernie especially was dripping in diamonds. But what they were on the outside didn't influence what they were on the inside, still just small town boys with a knack for making money any way they could.

This newfound money and power wasn't enough for Big Carl. He wanted more. He wanted people to look up to him, to think of him as a businessman, to admire him for all he felt he had accomplished. He especially wanted the respect of the rich, powerful and elite with whom he rubbed shoulders almost daily. But he didn't get it. He was often heard to say that he was good enough for them to buy his liquor but not good enough to sit down to dinner with him.

The area where they were opening their saloons was called "Little Egypt," because in the 1830s settlers from northern Illinois came south to buy grain when their crops failed after a long disastrous winter brought about an early freeze and a late spring. Just like centuries ago people traveled to ancient Egypt to get food during famines and draughts. Later towns in Southern Illinois were named after places in ancient Egypt, such as Cairo, Thebes, and Karnak.

With mining towns growing up all over the Southern Illinois area, the saloons and gambling joints the Shelton boys ran were multiplying. The saloons were called "soft drink parlors" since the sale, purchase and consumption of alcohol was illegal. There was even a "secret code" for ordering the drinks in these places. To order a beer you had to ask for "Orange Crush." The Shelton boys' power grew immensely. The police in the towns around them couldn't begin to touch them, and from what I've learned through my research, most law enforcement officers at that time didn't *want* to stop the illegal trafficking of alcohol. It would have cramped the lifestyle of too many officials who were on the take. Plus, they often imbibed the illegal hooch themselves. The alliance between the Sheltons, Birger and Newman was a force to be reckoned with. There appeared to be no stopping their rise to power.

Just when the Shelton and Birger alliance seemed to be taking over all the liquor operations in Little Egypt they hit a major roadblock – the Ku Klux Klan! Not only were they against anyone who wasn't an American-born white Christian, now the K.K.K. became a law enforcement organization supporting prohibition. As the Klan moved into Williamson and Saline Counties they numbered about 5,000 members. By summer of 1923 the Klan was holding cross burning rallies through the towns of Marion, Carterville and West Frankfort.

When the Klan held a rally in East St. Louis that same year, there were 10,000 Klansman in attendant at the cross burning on a local farm. They next drove about 100 cars with white handkerchiefs attached through town at midnight as a show of power. As they passed the police station the officers ordered them to stop and when they didn't, police drew guns. Only one car stopped. They charged the six men in that car with disorderly conduct and fined them $5 each. Little could these Klansmen have known as they drove down Missouri Avenue, that the Klan was about to come to their comeuppance in Southern Illinois!

Chapter 7.
Battle with the Klan

In Southern Illinois the face of the Ku Klux Klan was S. Glenn Young, a former federal agent who had lost his job twice before with the Justice Department. The Williamson County Klan selected Young to direct their investigations into the growing problems of speakeasies and roadhouses that flaunted Prohibition.

Born in Kansas he grew up as a cowboy, herding cattle and always had a gun in his hand. He was always fighting, quick to shoot, asked questions later and seemed to be afraid of nothing. He had gone after draft dodgers during World War I and later became a federal agent, but when he shot and killed a man in a raid, he was suspended. By the time he was exonerated of the charges, other inappropriate activities during his career had come to light and he lost his job.

The Klan hired Young in the fall of 1923 and by November he and his hand-picked few from out of the county started visiting dozens of roadhouses. They ordered beer and whiskey all the while collecting evidence to take to the feds. When Prohibition agents viewed the evidence they authorized a series of raids using federal agents augmented with hundreds of Klansmen. The first raid came just before Christmas. Two more followed in quick succession in the new year. After the three big raids, 256 men and women had been arrested. "Williamson County was in an uproar."[21]

---

[21] Paul Angle. 1954. *Resort to Violence*. (British version of *Bloody Williamson*). London: The Bodley Head. 123.

Young and his men were raiding all the roadhouses in their path and confiscating all the liquor they could get their hands on, along with breaking furniture and the taverns too. In addition they stole money and harassed the Catholic immigrants in the mining towns. Victims made complaints to the French and Italian consulates. Finally the federal government backed off. Young, they determined, was too hot. That of course couldn't stop him. If they couldn't act under federal authority, they would do so under local authority. They found it in Herrin Township Constable Caesar Cagle, a bootlegger who figured the Klan would win in the end so he ought to just join them.

The problem with Cagle was that he had no morals about double-crossing. At one point during the raids a Klan leader found Cagle and Harry Walker, who would later join the Sheltons, unloading confiscated booze into Cagle's garage which he later planned to sell back to the roadhouses that had been raided. It's quite possible the liquor even came from the Sheltons themselves. Sometime in January 1924, Cagle and Young led a group of Klansman over to Colp and raided Earl Shelton's joint, the one he ran with Jack Skelcher. There they wrecked the building, confiscated the gambling money and all of the booze and slammed Earl up against the wall with gun sighted on him. Young wanted to know who the Sheltons were paying off. My uncles had learned how to buy off people, especially officials, so they didn't always have to resort to violent means to get what they wanted. Big Earl refused to answer. Cagle, with guns still pointed at my uncle, hit Earl with his weapon. When he fell to the floor Cagle proceeded to pistol whip him. They then dragged Earl outside and burned down his building.

This was Cagle's last mistake! The Klan had just made it personal. As Carl noted in later years, "them fellers ain't so much pro-white as they [we]'re anti-Shelton."[22]

The Klan continued to hold raids throughout the month and into February. On the 8th, when the Sheltons and anti-Klansman led by Ora Thomas learned about a big Klan raid planned for the next day, my uncles decided to hold their own rally in Herrin. They called together those who were sick of the violent infiltration of the Klan in their lives. They started out at the Rome Club in a second-floor meeting room with dozens who hated the Klan. Sheriff Galligan, an opponent of the Klan, arrived first with his chief deputy, John Layman. Before they could settle my uncles and everyone down, Herrin's three policemen, all Klansmen, arrived in the stairwell coming up to the meeting. Galligan, Layman, Thomas and my uncles got into the stairwell to stop them. A shot rang out and struck Layman in the chest. The sheriff quickly took the police officers away fearing for their lives. Thomas took Layman to the hospital. That left my uncles in charge.

By now the group was an angry mob and had moved outside. Someone saw Cagle's young son walk down the sidewalk. When my uncles confirmed his parentage they told him to go get his pa as Layman had been shot. While the son went off in one direction, the Sheltons and their followers took off in another. Regrettably for Cagle, they found him first. Big Earl hit him over the head with his gun, then Cagle was shot, several times. The mob disappeared as Cagle lay bleeding on the sidewalk. He was taken to the hospital by onlookers where he later died. The Sheltons drove away.

---

[22] Feb. 1976. *Official Detective.*

Young was in Marion when he heard of Cagle's death. He immediately sent enough Klansmen to overtake Herrin, as he headed there himself. They patrolled the streets, stopped traffic, questioned people, even put up roadblocks. If you didn't know the Klan password, you didn't get into the city!

Young found out Laymen was still alive in the hospital and attempted to reach him there. He was refused admittance to the hospital and this started an all out war for Herrin's citizens. Young and his men opened fire on the hospital. Those inside who could shoot back did, but it was a hospital with doctors, nurses and patients. The firing continued until early the next day when troops the sheriff had sent for arrived and stopped the shooting, but not for long.

Young was running Herrin! He had the sheriff and the mayor locked up. The state sent in troops from the Illinois National guard to establish peace. By February 12 things had started to calm down in Herrin. The sheriff and mayor were released from jail. The grand jury handed down indictments against Carl and Earl for the murder of Cagle, but the two Shelton boys were long gone, taking the rum runners' southern route to Florida. Young was indicted on counts of false imprisonment, conspiracy, kidnapping, parading with arms, assault with intent to murder, malicious mischief and intent to overthrow the civil authorities in Herrin and Williamson County.

The Sheltons soon returned to the county and turned themselves in to Sheriff George Galligan and filed $10,000 in bonds to assure their freedom. It was during this time my uncles really started focusing on growing their empire in East St. Louis.

On May 23, 1924, in Herrin the brothers watched from a nearby building as Young announced to a crowd outside he was heading to

East St. Louis to clean it up as he felt he had done for Williamson County.

Young and his wife left Herrin and drove toward their destination not knowing the Sheltons were following them. They drove through an area Pop told me about called the Okaw Bottoms, near the Kaskaskia River. He said this was sort of a no-man's land, an unpaved stretch of road that had no law enforcement anywhere around. He told me that if a person wanted to kill someone, this was the place to do it. My uncles apparently felt the same way. They waited until Young's car reached the Okaw Bottoms and then caught up to it. They hit the car with a hail of bullets, wounding Young and his wife, and sending their car careening down an embankment. One report said Young was able to get out of the car hid under it. After emptying their guns on their target, my uncles left the scene. Another car eventually came by and took the Youngs to St. Elizabeth's Hospital in Belleville, Illinois. Klansman guarded the room Young was in and patrolled the hospital to prevent the Sheltons from finishing what they started. Carl and Earl were charged with the attempted murder of Young and his wife.

On August 30, 1924, the court dismissed the charges against my uncles for the murder of Caesar Cagle when the only witness failed to appear. When everyone, including the Sheltons, left the courtroom, Sheriff Galligan and two of his deputies headed down to the garage to get the car my uncles were driving when they shot Young. After the attack Charlie Briggs and Jack Skelcher had stupidly driven it back to Herrin the next day apparently thinking no one had a description of the car. They did. At a roadblock outside of town Klansmen tried to stop the car. When it didn't, they opened fire killing Skelcher and wounding Briggs.

My uncles may have wanted the car back, but there was no way the sheriff was going to give it to them. Since the attack at the roadblock it had been learned that the vehicle had been stolen from a man in Cobden who wanted it back naturally. Galligan was off to pick it up. The problem was that the Klansmen at the roadblock had taken it to John Smith's Garage. Smith had become a major figure in the Klan and the organization had started to use his garage as their armory. The presence of the anti-Klan sheriff and his deputies could easily start a fight, but not even the sheriff could have predicted how rapidly the situation would deteriorate.

It stated with hostility, but still peaceful initially. One car of Klansmen pulled up, but they were disarmed easily. The second car though had a hot head in it who almost immediately put a bullet into the head of one of the deputies, Bud Allison. A second bullet grazed the other deputy, Ora Thomas, temporarily knocking him to the ground. For a moment the sheriff, a former police chief in Herrin who knew most of these men, was the only one left standing on his side. Quickly the first help arrived, but for the sheriff, it wasn't the help he wanted. It turned out to be his 16-year-old son who had been attending the trial as a spectator. He picked up a weapon and joined his father in the battle. Thomas re-entered the fight and about then my uncles joined the action saving the day for the sheriff.

By the end six men lay dead and a seventh mortally wounded, including, believe it or not, a Klan-hired gunman who had squatted down under a grape arbor across the street from the garage wearing a sombrero and spurs. The other dead included the deputy Allison, the Klansmen who shot him, another Klansmen, and two bystanders, including one pedestrian who was walking down the sidewalk with his wife and child in a stroller. The court bailiff, who was also a special deputy sheriff, and more appropriately for the county, a bootlegger as well, came running up during the last half of the battle. He was immediately shot in the head and would last days before finally succumbing to his wounds. Others were wounded, including Carl and Earl with minor injuries. It's not clear if the sheriff and my uncles were good friends prior to the shootout, but they most certainly were afterward.[23]

By January 1925 Young had established his own core group of Klansman that had carved out a portion of Herrin under their control. The county's Klan leaders had tried to get rid of him, but he just sent one of his gunman to Marion for a drive-by shooting of the man's house. The papers reported rumors he was going to take over the leadership of the Chicago Klan and give Chicago a taste of what he had accomplished in Southern Illinois. As his enemy list grew longer his life grew shorter. On the evening of January 25 a shot rang out in Herrin near City Hall. To this day no one knows who fired the shot or why. It drew both Young and Thomas to investigate at different times. A passerby shouted out an insult to Young who quickly crossed the street to the entrance of the European Hotel building. There he berated the man who entered the cigar store in the front of the building. Young and two of his bodyguards followed. Thomas, who was down the block saw the incident and entered the building from the side reaching the cigar store from the back. A shootout followed with Thomas killing Young, someone killing the bodyguards, and finally a third person shooting Thomas. In minutes the leaders of both the Klan and anti-Klan factions were dead. It looked like a set up, but if so, one that Thomas didn't know

---

[23] George Galligan and Jack Wilkinson. 1927, Reprinted 1985. *In Bloody Williamson*. Marion, Ill.: Williamson County Historical Society. 47-53; and Ralph Johnson and Jon Musgrave. 2010. *Secrets of the Herrin Gangs*. Marion, Ill.: IllinoisHistory.com. 14-16.

the details as he carried the wrong ammunition for the gun he carried that night. Some have said outside forces, whether Birger, my uncles or even hit men from Chicago, may have played a role that night. Either way, the shootout effectively crippled the Klan.

My uncles and Art Newman came down for Thomas' funeral. Earlier that morning a group of men robbed a mail messenger in Collinsville. That event, Newman and the funeral would all play an important future role for my uncles.

The Klan remained relatively quiet for the rest of 1925, but started to become more active again as the spring elections approached, dominating first the school and municipal elections. It was likely they would repeat their success in the partisan primary election coming up on April 13, 1926. Earl and Carl wanted the politicians they had in their back pockets elected but the K.K.K. had their own men running. On April 12, Carl met with Charlie Birger, Art Newman and "Blackie" Armes, a Shelton hit man, along with more of their men, to send the Klan a message. Cars filled with anti-Klansmen drove through the streets of Herrin. The Sheltons, along with Birger and their men totaled about 40 men riding in six to eight cars. Guns were being flashed at every stop. When one of the Shelton cars passed by John Smith's garage, Smith saw "Blackie" Armes take aim at him. He ducked just in time as the bullet grazed him, but this was the shot that began the end to the K.K.K. in Southern Illinois!

Bullets began flying everywhere, from cars, from people on the streets, from windows in buildings even in neighboring blocks. It seemed as if everyone in town was joining in the gunfight. The Sheltons were leading the attack against the one organization that appeared big enough and strong enough to take the Sheltons down! Carl had parked by the European Hotel down the street and seemed to be calling the shots. Bernie was among the shooters. The assault on the garage lasted less than 15 minutes. After the Illinois National Guard arrived and surrounded Smith's garage the gangsters drove off. Their message had been delivered.

Three of the cars though continued through Herrin towards the Masonic Temple where the Klan had its supporters standing guard outside a polling place. After one pass around the block they came back for a second swing. The cars stopped and what became known as the Election Day Riot took place. The cars held a number of gangsters including Carl, and probably Earl and Bernie, along with at least Charlie Briggs, "Jardown" Armes, and other members of the Shelton side. Birger was there with his top lieutenant Aub Treadway and Noble Weaver, an underworld boss from neighboring Franklin County.

The Klan was prepared and the death toll was even with three dead on both sides. The Sheltons lost Briggs, Birger lost Treadway and the Franklin County underworld lost Weaver. The latter two deaths would create big holes to fill. The men who filled them, Art Newman and Joe Adams, would cause more trouble than they were worth.

There hasn't been much that I have found out about my uncles that I can be, I guess you would say, "proud of," but if there is, this would be it. My uncles led an assault against a most prejudiced and violent organization. Having grown up in the deep South, I have had the most unpleasant experience of witnessing K.K.K. crosses on the lawns of good people who are simply trying to make a better life for themselves and their families. I know the Sheltons didn't attack the Klan to help anyone but themselves. If their liquor business had not been in danger they would never have looked twice, but, motive aside the results were the same, my uncles ran the Ku Klux Klan out of Southern Illinois!

Chapter 8.
End of an Alliance

After the death of S. Glenn Young in January 1925 the rest of the year proved relatively uneventful. There were the occasional bombings and shootings between Klan and anti-Klan forces, but nothing like the mass shootouts in the streets from the year before. Up in East St. Louis Art Newman finally wore out his welcome in February and my uncles tried to have him killed. He shot the shooter instead, but realized it would be safer for him to relocate. He took his wife along with his employee Freddie Wooten, who had been shot the previous November, and headed for points south.

Now that the Klan was nearly out of the picture the Sheltons and Charlie Birger had nothing to stand in the way of their rise to power, wealth and fame. Nothing, of course, but themselves. In December my uncles and Birger reached an agreement over gambling. From then on, they would jointly operate the slot machines in Williamson, and probably other neighboring counties. Fifty percent would stay with the host establishment and the other fifty would be split between the gangs.

The problem developed that the more powerful they each became the more distrust the Sheltons had for Birger and Birger for the Sheltons. In February 1926 the state's attorney filed an injunction against slot machines that last for a week or so. After it lifted Birger picked one of his guys to do the collecting. From that point forward the Sheltons noticed their take diminishing. Earl thought Birger was skimming more than his share of the take. He was, though it was probably to pay off the state's attorney. He just took it from my uncles' portion rather than his. Still, with the booze and gambling in the roadhouses and now the slot machines all over, their haul was ever increasing.

Though they stood together against the K.K.K. and often worked together, each side still each had its own territories to run their roadhouses and sell their booze. They each had their own loyal men working for them. Competition and rivalry only added to the mistrust between the two factions. After the Election Day Riot in April soon the line in the sand was drawn. There was no more Shelton-Birger alliance. You were on Charlie Birger's side or you were on the Shelton's side. There was no middle ground.

What broke this alliance? Some people believe it was an all out turf war. Some think it was Birger's bookkeeping tactics. Others say a woman was their downfall, Helen Holbrook, to be exact. She was a beautiful, blonde, rich woman who lived in an old mansion over in Shawneetown. Helen loved flaunting her money and driving fast cars. Unfortunately for her, the lifestyle she adored included surrounding herself with rich, powerful, if not dangerous men. For Southern Illinois in the late 1920s the two richest and most powerful men were Carl Shelton and Charlie Birger, and according to the stories she was involved with both Birger and Carl at the same time.

Things started getting dangerous that summer. In July Birger and four or five of his men found Carl eating dinner at a roadhouse known as Shaw's Garden between Johnston City and West Frankfort. Birger entered the building with his men following and walked up to Carl and demanded, "What have you got against me?" Carl started cursing and pulled his gun, "Charlie... I ought to kill you." The two argued and Carl eventually left with his men. For the time, violence would be averted.[24] It wouldn't be for long.

On August 22, Ray Walker's brother Harry and Everett Smith, another ex-con working with the Sheltons, were killed in a shootout at the roadhouse north of Marion. Initial reports said the two had dueled, but it more and more began to look like an attack on them both.[25] Five days later, Herrin officials who were allied with the state's attorney and Birger raided the Palace Hotel and arrested three of the gang members and "confiscated by the police some 25 to 30 pistols, a number of sawed off shot guns and several rifles equipped with silencers." While the gangsters bonded out, the city kept the weapons.[26]

About two weeks later Birger and one of his men ambushed more of the gang at a roadhouse outside of Herrin. "Wild Bill" Holland was shot and killed and the Shelton's business manager Max Pulliam wounded along with his wife.[27] Ray Walker and his wife were inside as well when it happened.[28] About the same time as

---

[24] Ralph Johnson and Jon Musgrave. 2010. *Secrets of the Herrin Gangs*. Marion, Ill.: IllinoisHistory.com. 41.

[25] Aug. 24, 1926. "One is Dead, One May Die Near Herrin." *The Daily Independent* (Murphysboro, Ill.). 1; and Ralph Johnson and Jon Musgrave. "Secrets of the Herrin Gangs." Marion, Ill.: IllinoisHistory.com. 41-42.

[26] Aug. 27, 1926. "Raid Herrin Hotel Arsenal." *The Free Press* (Carbondale, Ill.). 1.

[27] Sept. 13, 1926. "Herrin Again Kills, Robs." *The Free Press* (Carbondale, Ill.). 1; Oldham Paisley, comp. 2006. *Newspaper Articles from Oldham Paisley's Scrapbooks: Vol. 5 & 6, Klan-Young-Birger*. Marion, Ill.: Williamson County Historical Society, 36; Sept. 13, 1926. "William Holland Shot to Death." *Herrin Daily Journal* (Herrin, Ill.). 1; and Sept. 13, 1926. "One Killed, Two Wounded in Herrin Rum Gang War." *The Evening Independent* (St. Petersburg, Fla.). 7; Sept. 13, 1926. "Herrin Again in Booze War." *Laurel Daily Leader* (Laurel, Miss.). 8; and Sept. 17, 1926. "Herrin Gang War Flares, 1 Killed." *Harrison Times* (Harrison, Ark.). 5.

[28] Jon Musgrave. July 10, 2011. Notes on interview with Vida M. Boyt, daughter of Ray Walker.

the shooting near Herrin, Holbrook's warehouse went up in flames in Shawneetown.[29] Within a week Holbrook herself would be drawn into a coroner's inquest regarding a dead body found outside of town, a dead body long remembered as "Smoky."[30] Although Holland was the one killed in the shooting, the target may have been Pulliam who had been the original collector for the slot machines and had figured out what Birger was doing. Two days later as his family transported him in a hearse from Herrin Hospital to his home in Benton, Birger himself led the attack on Pulliam's caravan. If it wasn't for his mother using her body to protect her son from Birger's blows, Pulliam likely would have been killed that day as well.[31]

By this point my uncles had lost three men and had a fourth seriously wounded. A fifth would be taken out of action the next day when a federal court sentenced "Blackie" Armes to Leavenworth for taking a stolen automobile across state lines.[32] Two days later they'd lose a sixth, if in fact Lyle "Shag" Worsham was serving as a spy for

---

[29] Sept. 16, 1926. "Shawneetown Visited by Two Destructive Fires." *Gallatin Democrat* (Shawneetown, Ill.). 1.

[30] Sept. 23, 1926. "Finding Mutilated Corpse Mystifies Community." *Gallatin Democrat* (Shawneetown, Ill.). 1; and Gary DeNeal. 1981, 2nd ed. 1998. *A Knight of Another Sort: Prohibition Days and Charlie Birger.* Carbondale, Ill.: Southern Illinois University Press. 121.

[31] Sept. 15, 1926. "Pulliam Beaten by Six Gangsters." *Herrin Daily Journal* (Herrin, Ill.). 1; Sept. 15, 1926. "Armed Men Attack Pulliam In Ambulance On Way to Hospital." *The Daily Independent* (Murphysboro, Ill.). 1; Sept. 15, 1926. "Wounded Herrin Man Beat Up in Ambulance." *The Free Press.* (Carbondale, Ill.). 2; Oldham Paisley, comp. 2006. *Newspaper Articles from Oldham Paisley's Scrapbooks, Volume 5-6, Klan-Young-Birger.* Marion, Ill.: Williamson County Historical Society. 36-37. "Make Another Attack on Life of Pulliam;" Carla Pulliam, comp. 1998. *The Daily American, West Frankfort, Illinois, 1925-1926.* Privately published. 103; and Sept. 15, 1926. "Mack Pulliam, in an...." *Marion Evening Post* (Marion, Ill.). 1. Paisley Scrapbooks. Marion, Ill.: Williamson County Historical Society. 5-6:35.

[32] Sept. 16, 1926. "Blackie Arms Herrin Gangster Sentenced." *Carbondale Free Press* (Ill.). 1.

my uncles. He was taken out and machine-gunned south of Carterville and later had his body burned in an abandoned home near the south county line at Pulley's Mill.

That weekend saw the Great Miami Hurricane slam into Florida's Atlantic Coast. Among the refugees that fled the city after its wrath were Art Newman and his wife. Hearing about the developing gang war that had been picked up and reported across the country, Newman decided it was time to come back on the side of Birger who decided he could fill the role left empty by Treadway who had died earlier in April.

The arrival of Newman and his own personal henchman Wooten somehow exacerbated the situation even worse. When Holbrook saw Birger and Newman on the sidewalk together in Harrisburg, she immediately went home and called Carl to tell him the news. Uncle Carl made three attempts to call Birger warning him about Newman. Birger just laughed and probably told him something that isn't repeatable. By this time the Shelton boys had converted a gasoline tanker truck used to haul booze, into a war tank they would use to attack Birger and his men. They cut a slot down each side so they could line up in the back of it and take aim. There was a machinegun mounted in the back. It wasn't pretty and didn't move very fast. With Newman in the picture my uncles decided the time had come to debut it.

The next day they drove it through Marion and down Route 13 past Shady Rest looking for Birger. The closest they came to finding Birger was when they ran across Newman and his wife on their way back from Harrisburg. As the Sheltons drove their giant mammoth of a shooting machine they riddled Newman's car with bullets, missing Newman but wounding Bessie.

It annoyed Birger that the Sheltons had something he didn't so he took a truck he owned and had it lined with sheet metal. It took weeks to complete the job and in the meantime Birger laid low so his enemies wouldn't find him. This was now his armored tank. They would both roll up and down the highways looking for the other one. People who had to travel this highway even learned to find alternative routes to avoid running into one of these machines.

The Sheltons had fewer men than Birger. They didn't even call themselves a gang, that was a label put on them by others, mostly the press. They would refer to each other as the "Shelton Boys." Though after the debut of their "tank" they started recruiting more men from the St. Louis area Cuckoo Gang for help.[33] Birger had more men working for him and he loved the limelight! He went for the public relations at every opportunity giving interviews to the press and even inviting a photographer to come out to Shady Rest, his roadhouse a few miles outside Harrisburg, to photograph him and 15 of his men. That October they posed standing around Birger's car with their guns. Birger sat on top of his car, wearing his bullet-proof vest, carrying his gun. It was quite the photo op for Birger. That the photo can be dated to a month is due to Newman's presence in it who had just arrived as well as Ward "Casey" Jones. His body was found floating in the North Fork of the Saline River on October 26. That same day a farmer discovered the machine-gun riddled corpse and car belonging to William "High-Pockets" McQuay near Herrin. Although from Herrin and had been served time along with Ray

---

[33] Ralph Johnson and Jon Musgrave. 2010. *Secrets of the Herrin Gangs.* Marion, Ill.: 44-45.

Walker earlier in the decade he had "become definitely aligned with Birger."[34]

With Birger losing two men everyone thought my uncles and their men were responsible. Newman even told the press a couple months later that the Sheltons were responsible for McQuay's death. In fact, two of Birger's men killed Jones, one of whom, Rado Millich, would be hung for the murder a year later. McQuay's death remains a mystery, but the surviving Birger gangsters interviewed in the 1970s by Gary DeNeal seemed to think two of their own, Connie Ritter and Fred "Butch" Thomason, were responsible as well.[35]

The Shelton boys had been to the Shady Rest many times as Birger had been to their roadhouses, too. They would meet to divide liquor, spilt up the take, or plan who they would go after next, but this time was different, they weren't going there to plan an attack on the K.K.K. or decide how to divide the liquor. Both sides were out for blood.

Birger's log cabin sat in a grove of oak trees about 100 yards or so off the main road where Birger had a normal barbecue stand that had originally served as a front for his operation. The cabin was known for its more adult activities of drinking, gambling and loose women. Cock fighting and dog fighting took place in pits out back. Now it was a locked down fortress. Birger knew the Sheltons would be coming after him. After all, how many people really lived very long after a split with my uncles?

Back and forth the gangs would strike at each roadhouses and strongholds. Operators were told to pick sides. Neutrality wasn't an

---

[34] Ralph Johnson and Jon Musgrave. 2010. *Secrets of the Herrin Gangs*. Marion, Ill.: 47; and Mary Jo Moore. 2008. *Bits of News*. Privately published. 7:152-153.

[35] Gary DeNeal. 1986. 1998. *A Knight of Another Sort*. Carbondale, Ill.: Southern Illinois University Press. liii, 130-131.

option. Days later it was Birger took the upper hand and attacked a Shelton roadhouse near Herrin. Again the battle went on between the two forces, machineguns, rifles, hand grenades, all across a highway, people driving scrambled for safety. Later it would be the Sheltons attacking a Birger-aligned roadhouse. These attacks took place not just in Williamson County, but also surrounding counties.

The Sheltons soon moved their headquarters to West City in Franklin County, where they kept their armored car. The small village sat on the state highway just west and adjacent to the county seat of Benton. The community's mayor Joe Adams was a long-time bootlegger and roadhouse operator. After Noble Weaver's death during the Election Day Riot he seemed to take over the action in the county. When Birger learned that he had the armored car, he started encouraging Adams to give it up. When he refused he upped the pressure. This set up a perfect counter attack for my uncles. With Adams in their back pocket, needing protection from Charlie Birger, Carl and Earl now started a new offensive. They were now giving information to authorities against other criminals!

By the end of October and early November Earl had contracted malaria and was recovering in St. Mary's Hospital in East St. Louis. When he found out Charlie Birger told a *St. Louis Post Dispatch* reporter, he would "kill Carl Shelton if he got a chance." Big Earl simply replied to Birger's interview that "the Shelton boys don't boast like Birger does." He simply retaliated by ratting Birger out. Earl let slipped that Birger had two hot cars and a $1,000 reward was out on one of them.

Birger was so determined to kill the Sheltons that he started talking in code on the phone if he was mentioning them for fear his plot against them would be foiled. Carl was "number one," Bernie was "number two" and Earl was "number three."

While Earl remained in the hospital with malaria, Art Newman came up with the perfect plan to take out "number three," or so he thought. His plan was to slip into the hospital in disguise, find Big Earl and cut his throat! Newman and Freddie Wooten, another of Birger's men, had quite the dress up party. They both put on women's clothing, dresses, high heel shoes, right down to the stockings. They really dressed to the hilt for this adventure, including close shaves and make up. Newman wore an expensive Russian mink fur cape and Wooten wore a seal skin coat and a silk dress. Newman carried a very sharp hunting knife under his cape for the job.

Stopping at the front desk they were shocked to learn that Big Earl was listed under his own name! As they walked down the hallway toward his room they saw Big Earl's current wife, Anna Carlson, and another woman leaving. Newman had the idea now that if they followed the women, instead of killing Earl, "number three," they could find Carl, "number one. Their plan did not work out. Not only did the failed to find Carl, the St. Louis police found them instead. Newman and Wooten were questioned and released. They claimed they were just on their way to Nashville to escape the gang war, but their third partner Rado Millich was out on parole, and got sent back to the state penitentiary.[36]

This event showed the fallible side of my uncles. They always seemed to have the idea that they were invincible, that nothing would happen to them, they felt too secure in any setting. This would prove to be the downfall of the Shelton Gang!

---

[36] Nov. 4, 1926. "Southern Illinoisans Arrested in St. Louis." *Gallatin Democrat* (Shawneetown, Ill.).

Chapter 9.

Taking to the Air

By November 1926 the battle between the Birger and Shelton gangs had reached a new height. On November 10, someone in the gang threw a bomb from a car speeding down Highway 13 past Shady Rest. It was intended to hit Birger's barbeque stand out in front. The stand was spared but the windows in a nearby farmhouse were shattered.

The next day two pilots flew over Southern Illinois barnstorming. This was a practice of a lot of young World War I fighter pilots in the 1920s. They would travel around the country giving performances, flying exhibitions at air shows and fairs and even giving tours to paying customers. These two young pilots, unfortunately for them, suffered engine trouble and had to land at West City, Illinois, the Shelton stronghold controlled by its bootlegging mayor Joe Adams. Elmer Kane and Henry Mundale had no idea what was about to happen to them. From the moment those boys landed their plane in Benton they had no control of their lives.

Kane was flying a Curtiss Jenny, a World War I training plane. The Curtiss JN-4 "Jenny" two-seat biplane was never used in actual combat but instead served to train 95 percent of the pilots in Canada and the U.S. It was the first mass produced airplane. After the war ended a lot of pilots bought Jennys to perform in. This was how they made a living. While Kane worked on repairing his plane three Shelton gangsters approached him and Mundale. The flyboys were soon driven to get gas then taken to the home of Mayor Joe Adams.

There they met Adams, Carl and Bernie who immediately asked them about flying over Shady Rest and bombing it. How could they refuse? Not only were they offered $1,000 and a car if they agreed but I'm sure they knew the odds of getting out of there alive if they didn't. So they reluctantly agreed.

There must have been a lot of nail biting going on that night. The pilots had to spend the night at Gus Adams' house. Joe's brother who lived next door. Kane and Mundale watched as gangsters made the crude bombs of 20 sticks of dynamite and a two-ounce bottle of nitroglycerin "wrapped in a pasteboard box and tied with telephone wire" that they were to carry. I'm sure they thought long and hard about loading those bombs into the Jenny and all the different scenarios of what could happen to them, all the time wishing they had landed their planes *anywhere* but in Shelton territory.

Then, when everyone was probably just starting to get some rest, about 2 a.m. machine gun blasts riddled the house and one next door occupied by an elderly widow. Everyone hit the floor when they heard the guns start. By the time it was over Gus' home had been hit 29 times and the widow's next door 14 times. This was Birger's retaliation for the attempted barbeque bombing two days before.

Shortly thereafter six U.S. postal inspectors, the sheriff of Franklin County and one of his deputies along with a deputy U.S. marshal arrested Carl and Bernie Shelton on federal charges of holding up a mail messenger in Collinsville in 1925. After Carl checked the badges and made sure that the men were actually federal officers, he and Bernie gave themselves up. Everyone else went back in Joe Adams' house after my uncles were taken away.

Inside his house, after it got light Joe Adams gave Kane $1,000 dollars in cash and the gang drove Kane and Mundale back to the Jenny, which was being guarded by Shelton men. The plane was fueled up and ready to fly. The two-seat Jenny could only carry the pilot and someone from the gang to drop the bombs. The pilot would be Kane. The bomber would be Ray Walker and Mundale would be held on the ground as insurance.

They took off from the field and soon were circling about 400 feet above Shady Rest. Walker dropped the first bomb but it was to no avail. It didn't explode, but there was enough noise from the plane to arouse the interest of Birger's men. They came running out of the cabin holding their fire at first to make sure it wasn't a government plane, but when Kane made his second found the gang opened fire with their rifles and machine-guns at the Jenny. The second and third bombs were dropped. One of them also was a dud, but one exploded, hitting the cockfighting pen, killing an eagle and Birger's favorite bulldog.

Birger's men missed the Jenny completely and Kane flew to DuQuoin, where he left Walker. There have been many different ideas as to who the Shelton bomber was. I could find no proof about this, but it certainly wasn't "Blackie" Armes who often got credit in later decades as he was already in Leavenworth at the time. His brother "Jardown" and Walker called Birger and took credit for the mission later that day.

"We have just flown over your place and dropped a few of our compliments. How do you like it?"

The general assumption in the family was always Walker. Later I learned that he admitted to his daughter he was the one in the plane.

Kane then flew off to meet Mundale who was waiting at another airfield with their car. Unfortunately it was a *hot* car as it had been stolen nine days before from in front of a movie theater. The pilots were later arrested in Iowa and found guilty of interstate transportation of a stolen auto. They were each sentenced to sixty days in jail and fined $100.[37]

This was a most fascinating account for me because, first of all, the coincidence of the names. Both Elaine and I have daughters named Jenny! We had never met, did not know anything about the other except that we existed, and neither of us knew about the bombing from a Curtiss Jenny. I was the one who told Elaine the name of the plane that was flown to bomb Shady Rest. During a phone conversation we were talking about the incident and I said, "it was a Curtiss Jenny." Elaine turned to her husband, and asked him if he knew what kind of plane was used to bomb the Shady Rest. He said, "Yeah, it was a Curtiss Jenny." She laughed and said to me, "You got that from the Sheltons, your love of cars, bikes and planes." She was right.

But I guess the most important thing to take away from this account about Kane and Mundale is how quickly and completely my uncles' antics could change someone's life, for the good or the bad, but usually for the bad. Whether they wanted to or not, those pilots had no choice but to fly that plane for the Sheltons. To refuse would have meant their deaths; a fact they were well aware of.

The bombing of Shady Rest pushed Birger over the edge. With his opponents locked up, he worked up plans to get even with all his enemies, starting with Mayor Joe Adams. Just a month after the

---

[37] Nov. 12, 1926. "Airplane Drops Bombs Near Birger's Hut." *The Daily Register* (Harrisburg, Ill.). 1; Nov. 13, 1926. "The Bombs Were Crude Affairs." *The Daily Register* (Harrisburg, Ill.). 1; July 16. 1927. "Charge Flyer With Bombing." *Oswego Palladium-Times*. 7. Online at www.fultonhistory.com; Nov. 13, 1926. "Aerial Bombing Used in Herrin Gang Warfare." *Joplin Globe* (Joplin, Mo.). 1; Sept. 21, 1927. "Flyers Guilty of Bombing Resort." *Decatur Review* (Decatur, Ill.) 1; and Jon Musgrave. July 10, 2011. Notes on interview with Vida M. Boyt, daughter of Ray and Fay (Wollard) Walker.

bombing of Shady Rest, what played out on December 12, was to be the beginning of the end of Charlie Birger.

Elmo and Harry Thomason were two young orphan brothers in a family of five whose big brother "Butch" already killed for Birger.[38] The boys had just stolen a Ford roadster and they took it to Shady Rest to sell to the gang there the night before. They were just teenagers yet they sold out their lives for the $50 they were paid for doing Birger's dirty work. Soon one boy would be dead and the other would be sentenced to spend his life in prison. The boys knocked on the door at Joe's house in West City. Joe's wife Beulah opened the door and when they asked for Joe, she told them her husband was sleeping. They insisted on seeing him, saying they had a message in the form of a note from Carl Shelton.

Beulah reluctantly awoke her husband and he went to the door. They handed him a note.

"Friend Joe. If you can use these boys please do it. They are broke and need work. I know their father."

Signed, "C.S."

As Adams read the note, the two young boys drew their guns and shot him repeatedly. With no remorse or pain of conscience these two boys, having no idea that their lives had effectively ended that day, left the front porch with their murdered victim lying in his own blood. They ran off to a car waiting on them and drove away from the area. Adams lived for another hour. During that time he told his wife that he did not know the boys who shot him. Of course the note was a forgery. Its intent was to lure Adams to the door of his house. It worked.

---

[38] Gary DeNeal. 1986. 1998. *A Knight of Another Sort*. Carbondale, Ill.: Southern Illinois University Press. 130-131.

At the coroners' inquest, Beulah said Charlie Birger called several times the days before threatening her husband's life. On one call he even told her to take out more life insurance on Adams. She was going to need it, he said. With the efforts of Adams' widow and brother, Saline County authorities arrested Birger for Adams' murder, but ridiculously allowed him to keep his Tommy gun in the jail cell with him. He soon made bail and was back out.

Birger's insanity continued as the new year rolled around. The Sheltons faced trial for the Collinsville job at the end of the month, but Birger thought he needed to do more to move public opinion against his enemies.

On January 9, 1927, Shady Rest blew up and what was left burned to the ground. Birger, of course, blamed the Sheltons, but considering that he and his men had just days before, removed all their valuables and their guns, tells the obvious. Birger himself was behind the destruction of his beloved log cabin in the woods.

Found in the ashes of the Shady Rest were the charred remains of four people, one of whom was Elmo Thomason, the young man who along with his brother had shot and killed Mayor Adams. The other bodies belonged to Steve George, who was the Shady Rest caretaker, his wife, Lena, and another of Birger's henchmen, Bert Owens. All of whom could have testified against Birger in the case of Adams' murder.

Birger was clearly on a rampage and there seemed to be no stopping him. Just over a week later on January 17, a highway patrolman, Lory Price, and his wife, Ethel, disappeared. He had been close friends with both my uncle Carl as well as Charlie Birger, a little too close as it turned out. Birger was knocking off anyone and everyone who could testify against him or, it seemed, anyone who even looked cross at him.

Then on January 26, the body of Helen Holbrook was found in her apartment in St. Petersburg, Florida. She too had been close friends with both Birger and Uncle Carl, but closer to Carl in the last few months of the gang war. She was the "Queen of Gangland" as the newspapers dubbed, and was waiting for a Chicago reporter to arrive so she could sell her insider story. Max Pulliam had done so, and Art Newman and Connie Ritter were in the process.

Many thought she had been poisoned by the gangs, though by Birger's or the Sheltons' nobody knew. In the end the autopsy reported back as a suicide. She had drank a glass of water infused with chloroform in a room with all the windows and doors locked from the inside. My uncles may not have been responsible, but it didn't help when the federal prosecutor brought her name up in their trial and the possibility that she was murdered.[39]

On the day before the trial began the *St. Louis Post-Dispatch* started a series of articles with information they bought from Newman and Ritter. Pulliam' series published under his alias of Ralph Johnson earlier in the month in the *St. Louis Star* gave a generally accurate, if not occasionally vague, account of the Klan and gang war. The *Post-Dispatch* piece included Newman's and Ritter's alibis and misinformation designed to set up the Sheltons and protect themselves.[40]

---

[39] Feb. 9, 1927. "Mrs. Holbrook Declared Suicide in Florida. *Republican-Leader* (Marion, Ill.); reprinted in Oldham Paisley, comp. 2006. *Newspaper Articles from Oldham Paisley's Scrapbooks. Vol. 9 Birger-Boswell-Ritter.* Marion, Ill.: Williamson County Historical Society. 62; Jan. 30, 1927. "Says Mrs. Holbrook Killed Herself." *Decatur Daily Review* (Decatur, Ill.). 11; and Feb. 7, 1927. "Lay More Murders To War Among Gangsters of Southern Illinois." *Wisconsin Rapids Daily Tribune* (Wisconsin Rapids, Wis.). 1.

[40] Jan. 31, 1927. "Inside Stories of the Gang War in Southern Illinois." *St. Louis Post-Dispatch* (St. Louis, Mo). 3:19-20.

The Collinsville mail trial began at the federal courthouse in Quincy, Illinois, on February 1, and lasted for five days.

Birger, Newman and Harvey Dungey all testified against Carl, Earl and Bernie. Newman claimed he knew all the details about the robbery, that the Sheltons tried to get him to go in with them, that they tried to use his car and that he even walked in on them counting the money. Birger testified that he had a conversation with Big Carl about a "payroll job in Collinsville." He also said he came into his own house and found the Shelton boys and Charlie Briggs, who had since died, dividing up $3,600. He said Carl told him, "This is some of Uncle Sam's money." Birger said he asked how much they got and he told him about $21,000.

The worst testimony came from Dungey who was the one government witness that could actually place the three brothers in Collinsville the morning of the robbery. He said he saw the three in Collinsville while he was driving a taxi. He went on to expound about being shot at in the Okaw Bottoms the previous December by Carl.[41]

Not only did the prosecutor bring up Helen Holbrook which had nothing to do with the case, he also brought up Lory Price after Carl testified he had not talked to him since the previous year. That wasn't true and he should have known better. While out on bail and waiting for the Quincy trial, one of the gangsters drove Blackie Armes' car in Williamson County with Carl in the back seat. Down by the Herrin Wye they saw Price coming back from Carbondale with a passenger riding behind him on his motorcycle. They flagged him down and Price let his companion go into the nearby store as he

---

[41] April 28, 1927. "Says He Lied on Sheltons, New Trial Is Asked." *Carbondale Free Press* (Carbondale, Ill.). 1.

walked over to the car. There Carl had the last conversation he would have with his old friend.[42]

No one knows what was said but he was probably telling him his side had nothing to do with the destruction and murder at Shady Rest and that Price needed to be careful around Charlie. The warning came three days before he disappeared.

On February 4, the court found the Sheltons guilty of the mail robbery. The next morning before they were sentenced a farmer near Du Bois, Illinois, found Price's body in his field. It was a horrible scene. The body had multiple bullet wounds and had been mutilated by animals. Now the search was on for his wife's body. When it came time for the sentencing later that day the judge gave each of my uncles 25 years at Leavenworth.

How ironic that the one crime my uncles *did not* commit, they were convicted of. Even Agnes, their elderly mother was at the trial. She was brought by the Shelton boys' sisters, Hazel and Lula. Agnes cried openly in the courtroom as the sentence was read. As the Shelton boys sat in the bus heading to the prison they thought they would spend the better part of the rest of their lives in, they huddled together and cried. Uncle Carl's last words before entering the prison were, "We are here, and Newman and Birger have had their revenge."

As soon as the trial was over Newman ran. He was later found in California and during his extradition back to Illinois decided to tell all. It was a cold, rainy night January 17, when Charlie Birger and his men pulled up to Lory Price's house. Price came out and was told to

---

[42] Feb. 3, 1927. "Shelton Defense Rests Cast and Attorneys Begin Arguments to Jury — Shelton Story Rebutted." *Marion Daily Republican* (Marion, Ill.). 1; and Jan. 1, 1927. "Continue Search For Highway Cop, Wife Thought Kidnapped." *Decatur Evening News* (Decatur, Ill.). 2.

get in the car. He got in the backseat of Birger's car and as they pulled away Newman claimed Birger said to his other men, "Take that woman out and do away with her." Despite Price pleading for mercy for his wife, she was shot and her body dumped down an old mine shaft then filled with dirt, timbers, tin and debris. Newman led police to her body on June 13.

They took Price to the burned-out Shady Rest. Birger shot him three times. He wanted to dump the body in the same place as his wife, but when they got there a night watchman was on duty. Price wasn't dead yet and he was still pleading for mercy. All the time he could hear the discussion about what to do with his body. Birger wanted to burn him but it was raining too hard. They finally drove to a field in Dubois and carried him out of the car. He was blasted with bullets and left there.

Birger and Newman along with eight others were indicted for murder. Newman earned a sentence of life in prison. At one time a judge was asked what he thought of Newman.

"He was a killer. We characterize him as a thief, a gambler, a pickpocket, a hijacker, a robber and a murderer without a conscience… There is nothing that could be said in his favor and there is nothing that can be overdrawn when it comes to characterizing his wicked heart. He has murdered without pity, and without regard to sex; committing a murder seems to have no more effect on him than eating a meal, if he ever lost an hour's sleep by remorse of conscience we are not aware of it. We condemn him with all the fervor that an ordinary man can exert."

After much research, a very good friend of mine, a card playing buddy for the last thirty years here in Jacksonville, found out that he is related to Art Newman. The coincidences in the Shelton story continue to amaze me.

Chapter 10.

Turning the Tables

My uncles Carl, Earl and Bernie arrived at the U.S. Penitentiary at Leavenworth a day after their sentencing on February 6.[43] There they were processed with the standard fingerprints, mug shots and physicals.

All three had spent time in jail before, but usually just a local lockup or prison farm. Leavenworth would be the big time. A term of 25 years in a federal pen meant they wouldn't even become eligible for parole until June 5, 1935, that their minimum term wouldn't expire until November 19, 1943, and their maximum term not until February 5, 1952.

The winter must have looked bleak indeed for my uncles, but the days were getting longer and hope, like the lilies of spring, would soon break forth. The lies told by Charlie Birger and his men would come back to haunt them. The tables would soon be turned.

During the first week of March 1927, federal Secret Service agents arrested Riley Simmons and three others in West Frankfort for circulating counterfeit $20s. Simmons had been one of Birger's lieutenants. The bills had been made off of plates created by John Mayes and circulated through both the Shelton and Birger gangs. In fact, they were the same fake $20 bills that got Charlie Harris

---

[43] Carl Shelton (#27024), Earl Shelton (#27025) and Bernard Shelton (#27026) Inmate Files. Leavenworth Penitentiary Files. National Archives and Records Administration. Kansas City, Mo.

arrested and sent to Leavenworth when he used them to buy Canadian alcohol at Detroit for my uncles.[44]

By the end of that week on March 5, the Williamson County Circuit Court sentenced three of Birger's junior henchmen, Harry Thomason, Ray Rone and Danny Brown to long prison sentences after their convictions on robbery charges. They had been arrested after Christmas and convicted on the testimony of the girlfriends of Thomason and Ray "Izzy" Hyland, another Birger gangster. "They'll get a rope around their necks if we told all we know," hinted Jackie Williams, by then Thomason's ex-girlfriend, during the trial[45] Within two months she would be dubbed the "queen of the gangsters" by the East St. Louis press. Pearl Phelps, the other girlfriend, would have to settle for just the title of "duchess of the bandit court."[46]

In the aftermath of the trial at Quincy, Harvey Dungey soon had his fill of Birger. When the Harrisburg gangster made bail on the Adams murder charge, Dungey decided it wasn't safe for Birger to remain. On March 22, following Birger's release Dungey and three others snuck up to Birger's home and started "scattering gasoline" up against the structure. Birger and someone else with him heard the men and started shooting with both a revolver and a machine gun. Dungey was hit, but hid in a farm pond before finally escaping. That same month Dungey would later claim that Connie Ritter and Ernest Blue had tried to kill him at a roadblock south of West Frankfort. He

---

[44] March 8, 1927. "Connect Gangs With Passing of Fake Bills." Paisley Scrapbooks. 9:123. Note: The date stamp on this article is unreadable, but the article on the left was stamped March 8, and the two to the right were stamped March 11, and March 12; and March 9, 1927. "Counterfeit $20 Bills Sold For 50 Cents." *The Daily Independent* (Murphysboro, Ill.). 5.

[45] March 8, 1927. "Sentence Three Marion Robbers To Penitentiary." *The Daily Independent* (Murphysboro, Ill.). 1.

[46] A. L. Finestone. May 8, 1927. "'Find the Woman' and The Mystery Is Solved." *East St. Louis Daily Journal* (East St. Louis, Ill.). 2:1.

grabbed his machine gun and returned fire. Whether the assassination attempt came in response to the arson attack, or was the cause of the attempt is not clear. Either way if offered an opportunity my uncles could exploit.[47]

While at Leavenworth Uncle Carl quickly doused the flames of another potential flare-up. The gang's at least one-time business manager Max Pulliam had been picked up on a narcotics charge in Springfield and was out on bond. After being shot and then beaten by Birger the previous fall during the gang war Pulliam had become addicted to pain killers. His wife Mildred had done her duty and testified on behalf of my uncles at the Quincy trial, now they needed help themselves.

On April 23, Pulliam, his wife and another man, Pete Hungate, apparently held up a dry cleaners and laundry in Springfield. While the men wore masks Mildred didn't. Workers recognized her as the "bobbed-hair bandit" and police arrested her the next day. Max and Hungate high-tailed it out of Springfield and headed back to their homes in Benton, but managed to wreck their auto just a few miles away from the city, breaking several ribs and suffering other injuries. By the 26th, Springfield police were still questioning Mildred while picking up Max and Hungate at Zeigler where they had been arrested following the crash. As a known Shelton associate authorities could have put the squeeze on the Pulliams to tell more of what they knew about the gang's activities. That same day Carl wrote to "Pat Pulliam," Max's alias, and addressed it to a mutual

---

[47] Jon Musgrave. Aug. 8, 2009. Notes on Harvey Dungey drawings (#85 and #87) at the Franklin County Jail Museum in Benton, Illinois; and March 22, 1927. "Birger Routs Intruders Who Try to Fire Home." *Logansport Pharos-Tribune* (Logansport, Ind.). 6.

friend in Springfield. He knew there was change in the air and Max just needed to sit tight.[48]

The next day Dungey, who had perjured himself repeatedly on the stand in Quincy, signed an affidavit prepared by the Sheltons' attorney Edwin J. Burke. In it he admitted he lied about seeing my uncles in Collinsville the day of the mail robbery. With the confession in hand, Burke filed a motion in federal court to overturn the verdicts and seek new trials.[49]

For the Sheltons and their allies it kept getting better. That same day Springfield police released Max Pulliam and Hungate for their role in the laundry robbery after workers failed to recognize them. In a few more days, the workers would also change their story and deny recognizing Pulliam's wife.[50] Meanwhile the next day down in Harrisburg police and sheriff deputies arrested Birger for the second time for his role in the murder of Joe Adams based on Harry Thomason's confession to the Franklin County Grand Jury.[51] Later in open court Thomason pleaded guilty to his role in killing Adams. Asked why he testified, he answered because Charlie Birger "killed my brother" when he and others burned down Shady Rest.[52] Not

---

[48] Carl Shelton (#27024) Inmate File. Leavenworth Penitentiary Files. National Archives and Records Administration. Kansas City, Mo. Ralph Johnson and Jon Musgrave. 2010. *Secrets of the Herrin Gangs: An Inside Account of Bloody Williamson.* Marion, Ill.: IllinoisHistory.com. 74-77.

[49] April 28, 1927. "Sheltons To Ask Re-Trial." *Decatur Evening Herald* (Decatur, Illinois). 1; April 28, 1927. "Claims Perjury in Shelton Case." *Decatur Review* (Decatur, Ill.). 1; and April 28, 1927. "Says He Lied on Sheltons, New Trial Is Asked." *Carbondale Free Press* (Carbondale, Ill.). 1.

[50] April 28, 1927. "Pulliam Freed, Wife yet Held for Hold Up." *Carbondale Free Press* (Carbondale, Ill.). 1.

[51] April 29, 1927. "Charlie Birger, Gangster, Held in Murder Case." *Sterling Daily Gazette* (Sterling, Ill.). 1.

[52] May 1, 1927. "Birger Accused With Plotting Mayor's Death." *Joplin Globe* (Joplin, Mo.). 1.

only did his testimony nail Birger and Newman, but it also indirectly cleared my uncles in the burning of Shady Rest which had left four Birger gangsters dead. As Carl, Earl and Bernie edged closer to freedom, old Charlie moved closer to his eventual noose.

As one paper described it, "the coils of the law are gradually tightening around Charles Birger, notorious gangster of Saline County, who is now in jail at Benton, Ill. Deprived of his arsenal of machines guns, high powered rifles and the defection of former pals in crime, he has lost much of his braggadocio of other days, and it now looks as if several hitherto unsolved murders will be laid at his door."[53]

On May 8, Roy Shaw, another of Birger's allies whose roadhouse the Sheltons shot up the previous fall, earned his own trouble with the law. He ended up in a deadly bar fight down in Kennett, Missouri. After three men jumped him he picked up a stick of firewood and clubbed two of the men to death and wounded the third. He got away, but he spent the next year on the run through several states before being caught in Louisville, Kentucky.[54]

Four days earlier the federal court approved the motion to set aside the verdict and sentences in the Sheltons' mail robbery trial and grant the three new trials. All they needed next was to wait for Carl to recover from a hernia surgery on April 17. By the 14th he was ready to travel and by the 17th prison officials had received the orders from the court to take them back to Illinois.[55] Although they

---

[53] May 5, 1927. *Hardin County Independent* (Elizabethtown, Ill.). Online at Hardin Co. Odds & Ends pg. 2 http://members.aol.com/DeniseK322/oddend2.html.

[54] Mar. 2, 1928. "Man Sought Year As Slayer Caught." *Joplin Globe* (Joplin, Mo.). 1; and Carla Pulliam, comp. *The Daily American, Franklin Co., Illinois 1928*. Privately published. 15; quoting the May 2, 1928 edition of the newspaper.

[55] Carl Shelton (#27024) Inmate File. Leavenworth Penitentiary Files. National Archives and Records Administration. Kansas City, Mo.

were released for a new trial the government had no immediate plans to do so. "Friends of the accused say they will never be tried on the same charge. As soon as they are brought to Springfield efforts will be made to get them out on bail."[56] The brothers arrived back in Springfield around 5 a.m. the next morning on the 18th. Their attorney told reporters he would demand an immediate trial if the court didn't lower the bonds on the brothers from the $70,000 each required before the Quincy trial down to a more reasonable amount. Carl told reporters it would be a shame if a court ordered Birger to be hung for the murder of Joe Adams. Instead Carl thought he should be institutionalized. "Charlie is just naturally crazy. He ought to have to spend the rest of his days in a bug house. That's what dope has done for him."[57]

The same day down in Benton, Dungey continued to spill details of Birger and Art Newman's efforts to frame the Sheltons. The day or so after the Sheltons attempted the aerial bombardment of Shady Rest and postal inspectors arrested the three, Dungey explained what they wanted him to do.

"Birger and Newman suggested to me in the presence of others at Shady Rest cabin, Birger's gang hangout in Williamson county, that I join them as a witness against the Sheltons. I told them I didn't know anything about that job and asked if the Sheltons did it. Newman said, 'Hell no. But we can't trap them and we've to frame them plenty.' I told Birger I wanted time to think about it. He said: 'You will have to help. We could get Izzy, but we don't want him.' But I would not consent and left the cabin. About a week later I left

[56] May 19, 1927. "Sheltons Now Quartered in Springfield." *The Daily Independent* (Murphysboro, Ill.). 1.

[57] May 18, 1927. "Sheltons Out of U.S. Pen; Granted New Trial." *Carbondale Free Press* (Carbondale, Ill.). 1

some gin at the cabin for sale at Birger's barbecue and as I was getting in my car to leave Freddie Wooten came out of the cabin and took me inside. Birger, Newman and Connie Ritter were there, and Birger said, 'Now Dungey, you've got to help us frame the Sheltons on this Collinsville job. You're around here all the time, and you've got to go through with us.' I told him I didn't want to do this thing and Newman said, 'We're going to lie plenty, and you've got to with us.' Birger then told Wooten to take me to Harrisburg, before post office inspectors there, and we went in my car. When the post office inspectors started questioning me I denied I knew anything about the robbery. They talked to me about an hour and I still denied it. Then, I noticed Wooten in the room, fixing his eyes on me, and I knew it would be all off with me if I didn't frame the boys, so I finally told the post office inspectors I saw the Shelton boys in Collinsville the morning of the robbery. I did not see them there and I knew Birger and Newman would give me a machine-gunning if I refused to be a witness for them."[58]

While waiting for the court to set bail the Sheltons learned that Newman had been arrested out in Long Beach, California, on May 23, and would soon be heading back to Benton to stand trial for his role in setting up the murder of Joe Adams.[59] The next day Bond County prosecutors announced indictments had also been returned against Newman and four other members of Birger's gang for robbing the Bond County State Bank at Pocahontas, Illinois, the previous Nov. 30, during the gang war. With prosecutors focused on Birger's unraveling gang, the judge set bonds for the Sheltons the

---

[58] May 20, 1927. "Reveals How Birger Framed the Sheltons." *Carbondale Free Press* (Carbondale, Ill.). 3.

[59] Paul M. Angle. 1952. *Bloody Williamson: A Chapter in American Lawlessness.* 1952. New York: Alfred A. Knopf. 235.

day later on the 25th. The court agreed to set bonds at the lower amounts of $25,000 each.

"A delegation of Southern Illinois residents came to Springfield and signed the bonds." Four Southern Illinois businessmen and their wives pledged the total bonds of $75,000 secured by more than $170,000 in property.

Two of the men, Joe Kuca of West Frankfort and Thomas Bell, a retired merchant of Johnston City, had also pledged bonds earlier in the year for Charlie Birger. John Rolando, who owned a taxi cab service in Herrin and Emil Moroni, another Johnston City merchant pledged the rest.[60] Those two would eventually follow the Sheltons to Leavenworth themselves, Rolando for violating Prohibition laws and Moroni for bankruptcy fraud. Kuca, who operated the West Frankfort Bottling Co. and had worked with both the Sheltons and Birger in their bootlegging business, ended up himself in the Southern Illinois Penitentiary at Menard as an accessory to murder a few years later.[61]

The brothers returned to East St. Louis later that night. An Associated Press reporter tracked them down the next morning. Carl and Earl were still asleep but he found Bernie wide awake. "It's mighty good to be a free man again," he told the reporter. "We felt all the time that we had been framed. Prison life is not so bad. Carl and I were together as stone masons so we saw each other a great

[60] May 26, 1927. "Shelton Brothers Freed on Bonds." *The Edwardsville Intelligencer* (Edwardsville, Ill.). 2

[61] March 29, 1929. "State Briefs." *Sterling Daily Gazette* (Sterling, Ill.). 1; Emil Moroni (#32774) Inmate File. Leavenworth Penitentiary Files. National Archives and Records Administration. Kansas City, Mo.; Jon Musgrave. Oct. 17, 2011. Notes on phone interview with Tim Kuca, grandson of Joe Kuca of West Frankfort; and April 10, 1932. "Wayne County." County Intake Registers. Menard Correctional Center. Illinois State Archives.

deal." When asked about the murder charges facing Birger and Newman Bernie didn't show much sympathy, "looks like Mr. Birger and Mr. Newman are in bad. I wonder how they feel now." The article quoted Carl Shelton, possibly from the night before, branding as "bunk" a report from California that the three of them would be heading out to Long Beach to kill Newman. "Somebody is having a pipe dream and it sounds like Art Newman, who likes to play the grandstand."[62]

A couple weeks later two of the brothers and presumably Bernie's wife drove down to Benton on June 6, one day after their nemesis Art Newman had been booked into the Franklin County Jail following his capture in California. Bernie and Earl called on county officials and assured them they weren't, "looking for trouble." They were just there to call on the family of Joe Adams and his brother Gus.[63] From there they traveled down the highway to Johnston City where they stayed that night with the parents of Bernie's wife. They told a local reporter they didn't bear Birger any ill will but hoped "it costs him as much to defend himself as it did us... Those lawyers don't mind telling you two thousand for this and two thousand for that," they complained. "It has just about cleaned us but we're going to start all over and go straight."[64]

The following week searchers found the remains of Ethel Price, the slain wife of highway patrolman Lory Price. Just as Helen Holbrook's death haunted the Sheltons during their trial in Quincy,

---

[62] May 26, 1927. "All Shelton Brothers Out." *Carbondale Free Press* (Carbondale, Ill.). 1.

[63] June 6, 1927. "Newman, Birger in Jail at Benton, Ritter Is Sought." *St. Louis Post-Dispatch* (St. Louis, Mo). Shelton and Birger Gang War. Box 7/4. Carl R. Baldwin Papers. Southern Illinois University-Edwardsville.

[64] June 7, 1927. "Sheltons Complain of High Lawyer Fees." *Edwardsville Intelligencer* (Edwardsville, Ill.). 1.

the deaths of Lory and Ethel changed how the public looked at the gangs. More than anything, it sent Birger to the gallows. Prosecutors tried him, Newman and Ray "Izzy the Jew" Hyland for the murder of Joe Adams. The jury found all three men guilty and sentenced Birger himself to die for the crime.

On April 19, 1928, Charlie Birger wore a suit and tie and had a smile on his face as he climbed the steps to the gallows that held the swaying noose that would soon be around his neck. He stepped forward and looking at the crowd of hundreds, public relations to the end, said, "It is a wonderful world." At 9:48 a.m. Charlie Birger became the next to last man legally hanged in the state of Illinois, and the last whose death was a public spectacle.

Photo courtesy of Jimmy Zuber

GOOD TIMES – Earl (left) and Carl Shelton pose with an unidentified female, possibly their sister Lula in this photogrraph from the early 1920s.

Chapter 11.

The Life Behind the Big Time

The war between Charlie Birger and the Sheltons had not only left them incarcerated in federal prison, but all but broke financially. They had nothing to do but start over. And that's exactly what they did! Going straight though never had a chance. The next operation they would get their fingers in would be gambling. Big Earl started back running the booze. Big Carl organized the gambling situation that was already operating illegally throughout southern Illinois. They offered protection to gambling establishment owners against legal authorities and other gangsters. For this protection the owners would give the Sheltons part ownership and a lucrative cut of the week's take. The owners had to take the offer or they were out of business, forcibly.

When the U.S. Senate began hearings in 1951 about the rise of organized crime in interstate commerce, part of the testimony focused on my uncles' role in Illinois.

"With the collapse of the Birger gang the Sheltons were in full control in Illinois, and this control extended to the Chicago area. Law enforcement authorities have been of the opinion that the Sheltons were associated with the Capone mob at this time. Shelton had moved into the gambling business in a large way and was unmolested by Illinois authorities and instituted the payment of 'ice' to the authorities."

"A careful estimate of their income at the peak of their success in 1930 was that they were collecting $2,000,000 a year from slot machines, $1,500,000 from handbooks, and $1,000,000 from other gambling, such as dice, etc., and $250,000 from vice. Estimates were that they had collected approximately $5,000,000 a year, and after paying for protection and other costs of operation the Sheltons netted between $1,500,000 to $2,000,000 each year."[65]

Five million dollars a year, and that's before the illegal liquor take. I can't even fathom that much money. And where did it all go? They spent it! The Shelton boys loved the lavish lifestyle their newly acquired riches allowed them. But they were also very generous to others. They took care of their own. Be it family members or Wayne County residents who had fallen on hard times, they could never be called selfish.

One old acquaintance of Carl's that didn't fare well was Helen Holbrook, the woman that added fuel to the fire in the break between Charlie Birger and Carl. She had been living in St. Petersburg, Florida, when on January 26, 1927, she was found dead in a locked room of her home. She had been poisoned. A coroner's jury ruled her death a suicide. No one where she was from believed it was suicide. Everyone thought she had been murdered.

Arthur Carl McDonald was arrested in St. Louis on February 10, and questioned about her death. He told authorities that he did not know her and only knew the Shelton boys because of dating their sister, Hazel. He was later released. Hazel married McDonald, who was from Daytona Beach, Florida, in 1927. She was a court stenographer but her husband worked for the other side of the law. I was told by family members that McDonald was employed by the

---

[65] Special Committee to Investigate Organized Crime in Interstate Commerce. 1951. *Investigation of Organized Crime in Interstate Commerce. Part 4-A, Missouri.* Washington, D.C.: United States Government Printing Office. 812.

Sheltons. It was his job to make sure to make sure their slot machines worked... in the Sheltons' favor that is.

In 1929 Big Carl was again back in court. This time he had Renard, his stepson from when he was married to Marguerite Bender McDermott, with him. It's a convoluted case, but apparently Seburn Page, a Mt. Vernon, Illinois, youth stole a car in Detroit, Michigan, drove it down to Illinois and sold it to Carl. Then my uncle either sold it, lent it, or organized a highway truck robbery with it. I'm assuming he transferred it in some fashion to another set of gangsters lower in the gang's hierarchy. They used it on May 30 of that year to hijack a $25,000 truckload of *shoes* being driven from St. Louis into Illinois.

Interestingly the others charged included Josephine Wooten, wife of Freddie Wooten, and Joe Payne, brother of Bessie (Payne) Newman, wife of Art Newman. Also, Bessie herself was listed as a government witness. For a while it looked liked the trial would be a repeat of the Quincy trial and the subsequent Kinkaid bank robbery trial. Both times my uncles' enemies would tell whatever story in the witness stand they thought would hurt my uncles the most. The jury convicted the brothers in the bank case but the Supreme Court overturned the conviction. In the stolen car trial it was different. It would be Page and other lower-level gangsters who plead guilty and fingered Carl for buying the stolen car. [66]

---

[66] Sept. 13, 1929. "U.S. Indictments Include Some of Shelton Gang." *The Free Press* (Carbondale, Ill). 6; Sept. 18, 1929. "Carl Shelton Trial to Start on Sept. 24." *Alton Evening Telegraph* (Alton, Ill.). 1; Sept. 18, 1929. "Carl Shelton War Arraigned in Court." *Sterling Daily Gazette.* 7; Sept. 24, 1929. "Lindley Scores City of Effingham." *The Decatur Daily Review* (Decatur, Ill.). 4; Sept. 24, 1929. "Gangsters Turn States' Evidence." *Alton Evening Telegraph* (Alton, Ill.) 2; Sept. 25, 1929. "Shelton Case Up to Federal Jury." *Marion Daily Republican* (Marion, Ill.). 1; and July 26, 1930. "E. St. Louis Begins Drive to Exile Shelton Brothers." *Decatur Evening Herald.* (Decatur, Ill.). 1.

After 60 hours of deliberations the jurors ended up a hung jury and were dismissed. Prosecutors promised a second trial. By the time it started in March 1931, Carl faced a separate Prohibition charge. While the jury in the auto theft case ended up deadlocked again, the jury in the liquor case found him guilty. The judge fined him $500 and sentenced him to one year in jail with the final six months suspended. The judge also placed him on five years' probation with the promise to lock him up if he didn't get a legitimate job. [67]

The judge in that case knew who he was dealing with. That wasn't always the case with Carl who just didn't look or act like someone might think a gangster should. He definitely had the editor of the *Edwardsville Intelligencer* fooled in Madison County just north of East St. Louis. In an editorial a month earlier he defended Carl's reputation.

"Mr. Shelton, according to available information displays a really pleasing personality and has the appearance of a clean-cut young business man. Persons who claim to know him say they wonder about the truth of the stories concerning him. They wonder if he is really as bad as he is painted. Truly a most interesting character, in any event."[68]

While Carl spent time in the local jail up in Illinois, Big Earl focused on running liquor down in Florida. It was all part of a larger operation of smuggling liquor from the West Indies to south Florida,

[67] Sept. 27, 1929. "Jury in Case of Carl Shelton Disagree." *Freeport Journal-Standard* (Freeport, Ill.). 6; Sept. 28, 1929. "Baker Announces Shelton Will Be Tried Again." *Marion Daily Republican* (Marion, Ill.). 1; March 27, 1931. "Carl Shelton Faces Auto Theft Charge." *Alton Evening Telegraph* (Alton, Ill.). 1; and March 31, 1931. "Carl Shelton Freed in Auto Theft, Warned." *Decatur Herald* (Decatur, Ill.). 1.

[68] Feb. 7, 1931. "Concerning Mr. Carl Shelton" editorial. *Edwardsville Intelligencer* (Edwardsville, Ill.). 4.

and then back out to the Bahamas where it would be smuggled back into U.S. in various places on the Eastern Seaboard, including St. Augustine. It was there on July 24, 1931, the world learned of Big Earl's big vulnerability. While hauling booze from the Bahamas into Florida his boat ran aground in shallow water near the Crescent Beach bridge. Playing around in the rivers in Wayne County as a kid was one thing, but swimming to shore in the Atlantic Ocean as a middle aged man was quite another. Apparently even with all the time Big Earl spent in the islands and in Florida, he never learned how to swim! He thought it was too deep to wade out and so he and two other of his men just sat there in the boat along with their 830 sacks containing 5,000 quarts of liquor. They were soon escorted to dry land and arrested.

Authorities picked up another one of Earl's smuggling contacts, Fred M. Walton, sometime that year as well. Walton turned government witness and started testifying at grand juries about what he knew. In doing so he revealed another one of my uncle's smuggling routes. Although they had long used the area between St. Augustine and Jacksonville as a way to unload liquor into this country, after a decade of Prohibition the authorities knew it as well. In their search for new routes they created a new one direct from the West Indies to Camden County, Georgia, which was the first county across the state line from Jacksonville.

The local sheriff didn't mind as long as he got his $1 per case personal tariff. When federal Prohibition Agent E. W. Myrick picked up Walton he knew he had a golden opportunity to wrap up a number of long-time leads. Myrick had arrested Earl and a companion three years earlier near Troy, Alabama, with 500 quarts of whiskey and two revolvers, but for some reason was unable to see Earl prosecuted. Now he had the goods on Earl again, but first the feds would go after the sheriff. Tried separately that December the sheriff got two years for his actions. Walton testified that on one occasion the sheriff took $300 in fees, and the other $370. When a truck was captured with the smuggled alcohol, the sheriff sold it back to the smugglers for $200.

During this time Earl would be arrested in one city, make bail, then arrested again. At one point he was scheduled for federal trials in Jacksonville, Florida, Savannah, Georgia, and Mobile, Alabama. Eventually he was found guilty at Waycross, Georgia, on April 12, 1933, and sentenced to a $5,000 fine and 18 months in the federal penitentiary at Atlanta. He spent less than a year there as he was back in East St. Louis by March 19, 1934, where police arrested him for vagrancy. A month later neighboring Belleville police made it clear he wasn't wanted when they arrested him for vagrancy again on April 14. Local and federal authorities kept up the pressure and he ended back in the Atlanta pen by January 4, 1935, to serve the remainder of his term.[69]

Despite Earl's issues this didn't faze their business endeavors. The Shelton boys were on the fast track to all the money and power they ever wanted. The only other gangster who matched them in power in Illinois was Al Capone. Big Earl had a working, if not friendly, relationship with him. Capone had his territory and so did

[69] July 25, 1931. "Earl Shelton Seized Aboard Liquor Boat." *Carbondale Free Press* (Carbondale, Ill.). 1; July 25, 1931. "Shelton Held in Rum Raid." *The Southeast Missourian* (Cape Girardeau, Mo.). 1; December 17, 1931. "Sheriff Took Bribes Booze Runner Claims." *Thomasville Times-Enterprise* (Thomasville, Ga.). 4; Dec. 18, 1931. "Sheriff Given Two Years For Taking Bribes." *Thomasville Times-Enterprise* (Thomasville, Ga.). 1; April 9, 1932. "Shelton Ordered To Report At Savannah For Federal Trial." *Thomasville Times Enterprise* (Thomasville, Ga.). 2; Oct. 29, 1932. "Rum Smugglers Are Convicted at Trial in Waycross Court." *Thomasville Times-Enterprise* (Thomasville, Ga.). 6; and April 12, 1933. "Earl Shelton Gets 18 Months in Pen on Liquor Charge." *Thomasville Times-Enterprise* (Thomasville, Ga.). 6.

the Sheltons. The agreement was they would not cross into each other's area, they would not shoot each other's men, and they would split the liquor fairly when they shared a boatload from the islands, which they did at times.

This was about the time a new gunman went to work for the Shelton boys, a day they would live to regret, or, at least they should have. Frank "Buster" Wortman was a fire captain's son from St. Louis. He was aggressive, mean and a sharp shooter. He first earned publicity on Sept. 25, 1933, when he and "Blackie" Armes were caught attacking six Prohibition agents during a raid on a still near Collinsville, Illinois. They and other members of the gang were trying to rescue one of their own already captured who did manage to get away. The two were already definitely pals. On the last day of their trial bankers from Pana, Illinois, identified them as two of the four men who had robbed their bank on April 19 and stole more than $20,000. Sent to Leavenworth – it was Armes' second visit – the pair stayed friends and made a few more of their own.[70]

By the time they were released in the 1940s, they were taken into the newly combined organization by St. Louis and Chicago mobsters. This would later prove to be a deadly combination.

In the 1930s and early 1940s my uncles were at the height of their lives, money, power, they seemed to have everything they wanted. By 1940 the gang controlled practically every area in Illinois save Chicago, Cook County and "its immediate environs."[71] My uncles drove elegant cars, and most of them were bullet-proof. Their houses

---

[70] June 22, 1934. "Government Rests in Wortman, Armes Trial." *Edwardsville Intelligencer* (Edwardsville, Ill.). 1; and June 23, 1934. "'Blackie' Armes Found Guilty of Resisting Officer." *Edwardsville Intelligencer* (Edwardsville, Ill.). 1, 6.

[71] Special Committee to Investigate Organized Crime in Interstate Commerce 4-A: 812.

were the very finest that could be built and they were built with bunkers underneath them in case of emergency. These bunkers were at least 18 and as much as 24 inches thick, made out of solid concrete. Some of the bunkers, had tunnels a half mile long that led away from the house. This was in case they needed a quick getaway. The Sheltons were also known for their extravagant barns. With their love of horses, this was understandable. Uncle Earl's barn, that was later burned down, was valued at $7,000.

My uncles loved animals, especially horses and dogs. This is a love that has been passed down through the generations. Pop, Little Earl, their sister, Dorothy, and their cousin Jimmy, all grew up riding mules and horses. Jimmy told me that he and Little Earl would be racing Pop on their horses, and Pop was winning, they couldn't beat Pop. Then Dorothy would come running past on her little horse and she would always win. Elaine and I both have always loved horses. For many years, horses were a big part of both our lives. And we are definitely "dog people."

But things were not always fun for Pop, Little Earl and Dorothy. Even though they lived on the farm and were able to play on what must have been thousands of acres of land. They had room for riding their horses as fast as they could go with the wind in their hair and the sun on their faces, never having to worry about where to stop because the land seemingly never ended. The down side was that their parents did not get along – at all! Dalta had a temper, a very bad temper. I was told by a neighbor of one instance when Lillie took Dorothy and ran off to get away from Dalta. They were hiding out in the fields so Dalta couldn't find them. Eventually Lillie left Dalta while the kids were still young. That's why Pop was with the rest of the family so much. By the time Dorothy was old enough, she left Wayne County and lived most of her life in Alaska. Lillie soon was remarried to Roy Miller.

When Little Earl and Pop both came back from World War II their lives just melded right into the positions they had already been being trained for their whole lives. They were to be bodyguards for their uncles! Pop was already a sharpshooter before he left for the navy.

Pop told me he once had a picture of Uncle Earl in his new Model A Ford. He said Uncle Earl was driving it one day when he saw Earline McDaniel and another girl standing by the road. "Do you want a ride?" he asked her. Aunt Earline answered, "If you'll let me drive your car." Aunt Earline drove Uncle Earl's cars for the next 50 years! They were married on April 12, 1936.

Big Carl married Marguerite Bender McDermott in 1922. Marguerite had three children, two sons, George and Renard, and a little daughter, Alice who lived with Big Carl and her mother from the time she was about six or eight years old until she was about fourteen or fifteen. The boys didn't live with them, but later on Renard worked for Uncle Carl and was very close to him. In my research I found a picture of Renard's family standing on an oil rig with Uncle Carl in Pond Creek and on the back it said, "with Grampa."

Uncle Carl and Alice loved to roller skate together. It was one of Big Carl's favorite things to do. He had a skating rink built at his home in Peoria, Illinois, so he and Alice could skate together. As an adult Alice told her family about when she learned to drive. Big Carl taught Alice to drive when she was about 14 years old. They were in one of his bootlegging trucks and she saw a gun under the seat. That was just how things were in Shelton families, guns were always a part of growing up. Big Carl and Marguerite split up and the children were sent to a boarding school. The boys lived there until they were old enough to go into the navy. Alice went to live with her grandmother Genevieve Bender when she was about sixteen years old. Marguerite died in 1933 in an East St. Louis hospital from blunt force trauma to her head. She was 44 years old. She and Big Carl were still married at the time of her death. Renard went to work for Big Carl and became one of his right hand men.

Big Carl's greatest tragedy in life, even worse than losing his wife to death, was when he hit a small child while driving his car. He and Bernie were heading from Peoria to Fairfield. It was November 16, 1943, the worst day of Uncle Carl's life. He would gladly have given his own life for that day to never have happened. They were driving on State Road 121 by Decatur, Illinois. A little girl's life ended that day. But it had nothing to do with gangland fighting or guns. Little Violet Christine Varner ran out in front of Carl's car. She was only nine years old. Violet died from her injuries and Uncle Carl never got over it. He did all he could to help the family financially but nothing helped his conscience. It was not his fault but he suffered from feelings of guilt and nightmares about it for the rest of his life.

Big Carl loved children. He always had time for them, never a harsh word. Once when a lady and her little girl were walking down the sidewalk near Carl, the little girl fell and skinned her knee on the sidewalk. Seeing her fall and crying, Uncle Carl picked her up and carried her to a bench. After cleaning up her knee and wiping her tears, he gave her money to get an ice cream cone. Years later her mama told her, "That was Carl Shelton who helped you when you skinned your knee!"

Uncle Bernie spent a lot of time with a feisty younger widow named Carrie Stevenson in the 1930s. She loved the flashy lifestyle that Uncle Bernie had become accustomed to. They enjoyed life together on a ranch near Millstadt, Illinois. It was quite the party place which suited them both just fine. It also pleased my Aunt Lula. She was there a lot for the parties. Uncle Bernie named it "Happy Hollow." On the property there was a cabin for paying guests, a large ranch house for family and friends, a swimming pool and an incredible barn to house Uncle Bernie's favorite Palomino horses. Uncle Bernie and Carrie were also alike in temperament. This proved to be their downfall. One time in 1934 when Bernie had been arrested and was sitting in the St. Clair County jail in Belleville, Illinois, Carrie arrived protesting his arrest and demanding to be allowed to see him. The guards refused and she started getting physical. Eventually they placed her in a cell where she used her shoes to smash six prison windows. They separated or divorced in 1937.[72]

When Uncle Roy was finally released from prison he settled down in Pond Creek on one of Uncle Carl's farms. He married a woman named Blanche and they led a quiet life, at least for a few years. Between his stints in prison he worked he worked for his brothers driving cars and running liquor from Florida.

One very interesting person I learned about in my Shelton research was Callie (Shelton) Crews Fitch, the daughter of James R. and Tabitha Shelton. They were the family that took in Ben when his father gave him away after his mother died. Callie looked up to her older cousin Ben and was close to his whole family throughout her life. After Carl and Earl started making good money they opened a restaurant-tavern on Highway 15 between Albion and Mt. Carmel.

---

[72] July 18, 1934. "Woman Friend of Shelton Arrested." *Alton Evening Telegraph* (Alton, Ill.). 6; and H. G. Maynor. May 21, 1934. Report on Vernon C. Miller. File No. 62-872. Found in larger Charles "Pretty Boy" Floyd, Kansas City Massacre, 62-28915 Section 43 (Part 43 of 93). kcmassacre043.pdf. 120. The Vault. FBI.gov.

They served a little food, a lot of liquor and some gambling and prostitution went on in the back. On Saturday nights she held square dances there. At the writing of this book her brick house is still there. For years Callie lived there and ran the business.

Callie was a tough, independent woman. She would go for hikes in the woods, just Callie and her dog. They would stay gone, living off the land, for weeks at a time. She married early in life to a Crews but her husband died after just four years. Forty years later she remarried to a Fitch. She was so happy to be married to him. She said many times she wished she had met him forty years earlier. But that didn't stop the Shelton temper from coming out of her. I was told that the Greyhound Bus ran past the restaurant. It made a regular stop in front of it on Highway 15. One night Fitch was about to leave and get on that bus and Callie told him not to go. Then she made her words stick. She pulled her hunting knife from the sheath she always wore across her back and threw it at him. She hit him square in the back! He was only slightly injured and soon recovered. Unfortunately Fitch didn't recover from the car accident he was in. He was killed just a short seven years after he and Callie were married. She died in 1972 in Albion, Illinois.

My uncles often bought their cars from Brown's Chevrolet in Fairfield. Uncle Carl went in one day to order a new car. But it wasn't your ordinary 1946 Chevy, he ordered it with all bullet-proof glass. When it came in, he wasn't satisfied with being told it was built to his standards, he had to find out for himself. Big Carl pulled out his pearl handled revolver and shot every window in the car! He then turned to the owner and said, "Sorry, but I had to make sure. I'll take it." The people standing around looked scared, but no one complained about the gunfire.

After Pop got out of the navy, Uncle Earl took him to Brown's Chevrolet to buy him a new car. Uncle Earl told Pop, "Pick out any car you want." Pop saw a beautiful, blue convertible. "Look at that one," Pop said. But there was about to be a problem, something you didn't want with a Shelton. The owner looked at Uncle Earl and said, "That car's done sold." Uncle Earl asked Pop if he wanted it. Pop said "Yeah." "He wants that one," Uncle Earl told the owner. The owner threw Pop the keys, and told Big Earl to come back in the next day or two and pay him. Pop drove that blue convertible around Fairfield with the top down, honking the horn and waving at people.

Uncle Earl bought Little Earl a four-door Buick. It was "faster than a snake boat," Pop said, "We did some runnin' around in that car. It was modified to be bullet-proof."

The Sheltons soon controlled the gambling territory from Peoria to Cairo, even into Kentucky and Indiana. But their headquarters was in Peoria. They actually organized the gambling there. They established the "Shelton Amusement Company." Jack Ashby was the manager and Big Carl brought Ray Walker in as a top lieutenant.

If the owners of any gambling establishments refused to join the Shelton organization Uncle Bernie stepped in. He and some Shelton men would trash the place and the owner. During the destruction of one business the police were called. The officers told the owner he had been having too much trouble and he needed a good partner. The officers told the owner to take the Sheltons on as partners.

This also seemed to be the time period that Uncle Carl and Uncle Earl started thinking more of their old home in Fairfield, and more specifically, Pond Creek. They were making all the money they could possibly spend and they were getting older, ready to return to their roots, farming. I find it ironic that the thing they couldn't wait to get away from when they were young was all they wanted to return to in the end. Pa Ben never knew that he did have an impact on them. He died March 18, 1944.

Big Carl opened the Farmers Club across from the courthouse and police station in Fairfield. It was a gambling establishment on the second floor above a café. "The cops always came in to play," Pop told me, "but not in uniform." Big Earl taught Pop to run the craps table, Little Earl dealt blackjack, and my grandfather, Dalta, ran the poker table. There was a box in the back of the Farmers Club that held the worn out dice. There were thousands of dice in that box.

They pulled in a good amount of money every night. It was Pop's job to count the money, which explains why he thought he was counting out stacks of money while under anesthesia. Jimmy used to sweep up after closing. But one night while Jimmy was sweeping, he found a $20 bill laying on the floor. When Pop found out that Jimmy was finding money on the floor he didn't let him sweep up anymore. Now Pop took over that job so he could keep the found money.

One day Big Earl said to my dad, "We gotta go to St. Louis." Pop drove him. When they got there they went to a big nightclub. They went in through the back door. "So many people you couldn't walk around in the room. Had ten people shooting craps in a back room," Pop told me. A man gave him $100 to shoot craps and told him, "I want back what you win." Pop said, "Okay, what's the most I can shoot?" Pop said he played just for fun. First he won $500 then $2,000 dollars. Then he lost eight or nine hundred. When Big Earl was ready to go Pop gave the owner back all his winnings.

When my uncles traveled between Peoria and Wayne County they had a favorite restaurant where they liked to stop and eat. Before they left, they would call the restaurant and tell the owner what time they would be there. The owner would close the restaurant so that my uncles and their men would be the only customers when they arrived. Then my uncles would pay as if the restaurant had been full.

On the last Saturday of every month Big Carl would drive down the highway looking for hitchhikers to take them for a good meal. It got so people started walking down the highway on Saturday nights, hoping Big Carl Shelton would pick them up and treat them to supper. Whenever he saw a soldier on the road he would pick them up and take them out to eat. Sometimes the soldiers didn't even know who he was, they just appreciated the meal.

When Uncle Carl visited Florida in the winter time he would always bring back to Wayne County a truckload of oranges. This was easy for him because he had bought an orange grove in Florida for his sister Hazel to run. He would take the oranges to the school and give them out to the children.

Uncle Carl built the house in Pond Creek that Ray Walker lived in. Walker was a hit man, he *always* had his gun with him. Anyone who knew him said they never saw him without his gun, *never!* To hone his shooting skills he would put honey on the wall in his living room to attract flies. When they would land he would pick them off with a pellet gun.

My uncles' business ventures were going very well but this was not the case within their organization itself. There was a man who had been with them practically from the beginning, they even grew up together in Pond Creek, who felt he had been wronged, terribly wronged by my uncles. Charles Bryan Harris, a.k.a. "Black Charlie."

Chapter 12.
Corrupt Officials

One thing helped the Shelton gang reach the pinnacle of power they attained – the amount of wealth they were rapidly acquiring. They saw their cash flow as a two-way street. They had plenty of money and didn't mind spreading it around. Many politicians would rather take the cash and look the other way then stand against the Sheltons.

In 1941, Dwight Green became governor of Illinois. He saw it that way as well. During his administration a secret meeting of gamblers and state officials took place in East St. Louis. If the money kept flowing state officials would look the other way when it came to gambling operations. As long as local officials didn't mind – and very few did – the state would unofficially, but very definitely, be wide open for gambling. The gambling operators divided into groups. One person from each group would collect the payoff money and deliver it to state officials. This system lasted for the next seven or eight years.

Big Carl and two bodyguards drove to the designated drop site each month. The meeting place would change every month but not how the drop went down. The cars of both Carl and the official accepting the payoff would meet at a pre-appointed place and time. Both cars would stop alongside the road. Carl would get out of his car and walk across to the other car and would then hand an envelope filled with $2,000 cash through the window to the official.

He would then get back in his car and both cars would drive off. This happened once a month, *every* month.

This all changed after Green lost the election in 1948 to Adlai Stevenson. When he took the oath of office as governor in January 1949, Stevenson promised to clean up the state of Illinois. He ran on a platform of fighting corruption, particularly big gambling. Everyone saw him as a clean, straightforward governor, but he wasn't, at least not at first. Not until he decided to run for president in 1952. He won the Democratic nomination that summer, but lost to Dwight D. Eisenhower. He ran and lost again in 1956.

After Carl's deadly ambush in 1947, the job of delivering the payoffs fell to Big Earl. By the time voters elected Adlai Stevenson as governor Earl was spending a lot of time back home on his farm in Wayne County. Uncle Earl considered himself "semi-retired." He figured he could still manage the multi-million dollar organization from his farm in Pond Creek, but now he needed the next generation of the Shelton Gang to step up and take their rightful place in the business!

Earl now started delegating some of the jobs he and Carl had been performing for so many years to the nephews. Carl, Earl and Bernie had all married several times but they never had any children with their wives. This was in spite of the fact that my uncle Carl loved children. The only sons of Ben Shelton to have children were Roy and Dalta. Roy's sons had been taken by their mother when they were still practically babies to live with family in Chicago when Roy went to prison. This left only Dalta's two boys, "Little Earl" and my dad, "Little Carl," as well as Lula's son, Jimmy Zuber, to carry on the family business.

Big Earl decided the first job to be delegated to the nephews would be delivering the payoffs to public officials. Because Pop and

Little Earl mostly worked as bodyguards for Big Earl, this job mostly fell to Jimmy.

On one of my visits with Jimmy and his wife Barbara at their lakefront home here in Florida, he told me about delivering the payoffs. It started when he was young, about 17 or 18 years old, taking the payoffs to the sheriff and police chief in Fairfield. He thought nothing of it. He just did as he was told.

Jimmy told me of another payoff that nearly floored me. Our uncle Earl sent him to Stevenson's office with a payoff!

"Was it, maybe, Governor Green?" I asked since we knew he had been on the take and was greatly involved with the mob. I told him I had to know if he was sure of the name.

"Are you sure it wasn't Governor Green?" I asked again.

Jimmy got very serious. "It was Adlai Stevenson!" he answered.

He told me how it happened. He walked in with an envelope full of cash in his hand and he handed it to the governor. Stevenson took it and Jimmy left the office. He said he did this a few times.

"Nobody is going to believe you when you tell this because Stevenson was supposed to be clean. Everybody thought he was clean, but he wasn't!" he warned me.

Then he laughed as he told me about one of the times he walked into Stevenson's office. The governor had his feet up on his desk with the bottoms of his shoes exposed. He had holes in the soles of his shoes! After more research into Adlai Stevenson, I found that others noticed the holes as well, which was particularly odd since he came from a very wealthy family. Photographer William M. Gallagher of the *Flint Journal* took a picture of Stevenson's shoes at a Labor Day rally during the campaign. The picture became a sensation and Gallagher won the Pulitzer Prize for it the next year!

After Big Earl and the rest of the Sheltons left Illinois in 1951, he requested federal protection from Stevenson. He wanted guards at his farm in Pond Creek so he could return and farm his land. The fact that the Sheltons had Stevenson in their back pocket, at least during the beginning of his governorship, was probably why Uncle Earl felt comfortable and confident to make this request. He was comfortable because he and Stevenson had a working relationship, Earl sent the money and Stevenson looked the other way when it came to the Shelton Gang's illegal activities. Earl was confident Stevenson would accommodate his request because he was "Big Earl of the Shelton Gang," and, for the most part, got what he wanted from elected officials. Stevenson had already proven he could be bought, but not this time. By the time the Sheltons had left Wayne County, Stevenson had his eyes on a bigger prize, the presidency of the United States.

Although the Sheltons and Capone's Syndicate had a better relationship with Governor Green, it would be the corruption of a local state's attorney in Peoria Co., Illinois, that would bring everything out in the open and start the change in the public's attitude about the illegal casinos and nightclubs.

Unbeknownst to Bernie's killer, his influence on underworld dealings would not end with his death. It all started with a barroom brawl, something Bernie was very familiar with. A man who had way too much to drink was thrown out of the Parkway tavern. Another man, Richard Murphy, didn't want him thrown out and stepped into the altercation in the parking lot. Bernie, who never in his life liked to be told what to do, pistol-whipped Murphy with help from two Shelton henchmen, Ray Walker and John E. Kelley. The result came on June 25, 1948, when the Peoria County grand jury indicted Bernie, Walker and Kelley on charges of assault with intent to kill.

Roy P. Hull, state's attorney of Peoria County, just hated the Sheltons, especially Bernie! He pushed the grand jury to deliver the indictments. Hull had run for re-election in the spring primary election and lost. He blamed the Sheltons and the gambling organization as a whole for the defeat.

Now Bernie had a felony charge looming over his head and he needed to get rid of it. It was a bad time for the Shelton empire with the recent death of Big Carl, and there remained a price out on the heads of Bernie, Earl and Walker. Going to prison for a barroom brawl would have been a death sentence for Bernie.

Word arrived at the Shelton Amusement Company for Bernie by way of Roy Gatewood. Hull would drop the charges against Bernie – for a fee. Hull wanted $25,000. I guess that's what Hull thought losing the election was worth to him. Not to Bernie. He was mad, very mad! He told Jack Ashby, manager of the amusement company and one of the Shelton's men, about the offer. Ashby had worked with radios while in the army. He had an idea to wire Bernie's house for sound and record the conversation between Bernie and Gatewood.

Ashby bought the equipment necessary for the job. He took it to Bernie's house the next day. He decided the sun porch would be the most inconspicuous place to set it up. He put a table model radio on a table that had three seats. Bernie's wife, Genevieve, put a very heavy sewing machine on one of the chairs so the two men would have to sit across from each other and talk over the radio. Ashby put the microphone in the radio and ran the wire through a window and into the kitchen. Ashby, his wife, Mary, and Genevieve monitored the rest of the equipment set up on the kitchen table.

Bernie arranged for Gatewood to come to the house that evening. All that was left for the espionage to work was to get Gatewood, who always met with Bernie in his car, to come up on the sun porch and repeat the conversation. Bernie had a plan. He took off his pants. It was a hot, summer day so this seemed natural. He told Gatewood he was too hot and to come on up to the porch and cool off. The scene was set. Now Bernie just had to get Gatewood talking, and he did.

After they exchanged hellos and common courtesies, Bernie told him he had been thinking about the twenty-five thousand.

"Do you suppose he made a mistake?" Bernie asked.

"No," Gatewood replied.

Then Bernie went on to say something that I think should have tipped off Gatewood that something wasn't quite right.

"You know, I have the darndest time with your name. It's a hardy. G-a-t..."

Then Gatewood interrupted and finished spelling his name, "e-w-o-o-d. Gatewood."

Bernie continued protesting that $25,000 was a lot of money before adding, "you know that he is framing me."

"Sure, I know he is framing you," Gatewood responded.

Bernie even had the sense to get Gatewood to identify the framer as, "our State's Attorney," they were talking about.

Bernie put the recordings in a safe and told his wife what to do if anything happened to him. After Bernie was killed she did what he told her.

On July 26 Bernie died. By the first week of August Big Earl came together with reporter Theodore C. Link, to tell all and expose the corruption the Sheltons had been a part of. The ramifications would reach all the way to the State Capitol in Springfield. It would outline the widespread corruption in Illinois including state, county and city officials. Instead of the Sheltons greasing palms and heads turning the other way, now the Sheltons were about to tell all and a lot of people would be very unhappy about it!

Link worked for the *St. Louis Post-Dispatch*. The *Post-Dispatch* had been reporting for years about the criminal activities of the Shelton Gang. Another of the *Post-Dispatch* reporters included Carl Baldwin. After Big Carl was murdered the paper sent him to Fairfield to report an any additional acts of violence that might occur while he was there. The family often saw him sitting in his car in front of my great-grandmother Agnes' home for hours on end. She got so accustomed to seeing him out there she would go out to his car and invite him inside to eat. She would tell him she had fried too much chicken so he might as well come on in and eat with her. Baldwin later described Link as the paper's main link to the Sheltons. "He was the chosen receptacle for their information."

The most important ramification of the tapes took place in the state elections that fall. Not only did Bernie's assassination make headlines around the state so did the follow up of the revelation of the recording. Rather than focus on the corruption Hull's allies in the state tried to get even with their own grand jury investigation of the Sheltons. When it indicted in late October not the corrupt officials but Big Earl, Walker, Ashby and the reporter Link, the condemnation from the press around the state came fast and furious, and public opinion swung against Green and his allies.[73] Everyone knew about the gambling around the state, and it was easy to ignore if you were so inclined, but when the spotlight focused on the underworld

---

[73] Frank Sturdy. Oct. 24, 1948. "Four Indicted in Peoria Vice and Gambling Probe." *Chicago Sunday Tribune*. 1, 3.

gambling and vice led to the exposure of the palm greasing and payoffs of many high officials, the domino effect may have even shaped the outcome of the presidential election. The infamous "Dewey Defeats Truman" headline in the *Chicago Tribune* came about in early editions when the paper relied on polls and their own experts to predict the race. In the end President Harry S Truman edged out a victory in Illinois over Thomas Dewey by less than 34,000 votes.

Photo courtesy of Jimmy Zuber

BEFORE THE FALL – Earl, Carl and Bernie Shelton (on the horse), help gather hay from their farms in Wayne County in this 1946 photograph.

Chapter 13.
The Next Generation

Pop and his brother, Little Earl, along with their cousin Jimmy, led quite an exciting life growing up. Running harum-scarum around Pond Creek for all three of them, to the time they spent in World War II for the two brothers, their lives were nothing short of astonishing. They lived sort of dual lives as children. They had the times they all spent with their grandparents, Ben and Agnes, being nothing but normal country farm boys. On the other hand they had uncles who were becoming the most well-known and wealthiest men in the county. Their uncles loved them and spoiled them, especially my dad. As the baby of the family they spoiled him rotten. Every time I asked anyone what my dad did for a living, the reply was always the same. "I never knew of him doing, anything, not outside of his uncles' influence, anyway."

But they had fun as kids. Pop told me of the time the three of them spent on the farm. One of their favorite activities was fishing. They would sit by the river and lose themselves in the day, catching fish, skimming rocks, just letting life pass them by. Barefoot boys with rolled up overalls, a dog at their side and a fishing pole in their hand. It's the same way my son grew up.

The love of fishing didn't end when the family came to Florida. Once when looking at some old family pictures with Jimmy and Barbara she asked, "want to see what they did every weekend?" as she handed me pictures of Pop and Jimmy here in Jacksonville. In every picture they had a line *full* of fish. They had just moved here after leaving Wayne County and were still living on my grandfather Dalta's land.

The youngest Shelton boys' other great love were their ponies. Pop named his pony "Blackie," and Jimmy's pony was "Pretty Boy." Pop, Little Earl and Jimmy would race on their ponies. Nobody could beat Pop as he ran "Blackie" as fast as he could. Then, Pop's sister Dorothy would come running past them all on her little pony. She would always win.

I have one picture I really treasure. It was taken on a beautiful summer day. Uncle Earl took Pop and Jimmy horseback riding out into

Photo courtesy of Jimmy Zuber

PONY TIME — "Little Carl" Shelton (right), rides his pony with his cousin Jimmy Zuber.

the countryside of Pond Creek. He carried a picnic basket with them, filled with the best picnic lunch you could imagine, fried chicken, fresh baked pie, all their favorites. This was the personal side of the Sheltons that few got to see, even fewer got to experience, the down home, country boy side of the most notorious gangsters the Midwest ever saw, Big Earl Shelton doing what he loved most, spending the day on his land with his nephews.

Photo courtesy of Jimmy Zuber

FAMILY PICNIC – Earl Shelton joins his nephews Jimmy Zuber and "Little Carl" Shelton for a picnic lunch on the family farm.

As Little Earl and my dad grew up, real life happened in the form of World War II. The time Pop and his brother spent in the war was horrific. Little Earl entered the U.S. Army 42nd Armored Division on November 26, 1941. He was shot in the invasion of Sicily and injured in an oil fire in the ocean. Terribly burned he survived as he in years to come would survive many assaults on his life. He received many medals for his heroism in the war, four Bronze Stars in the Sicilian, Normandy, Northern France, Germany campaigns of

1944 and 1945. He received a purple heart in 1943. He discharged on May 27, 1945.

Pop's tour in the U.S. Navy was none the less harrowing. He told me once, and only once, of a secret mission his ship was on. They were gone for six months and no one could know where they were. There was no contact allowed with the outside world during this mission. He said it was a very lonely time for all the men. Then the real trauma for him began. The ship went down in the ocean. He cried as he told me of spending three days in the water waiting to be rescued. He had to watch his buddies being eaten by sharks while he survived. He never brought this subject up again and neither did I. The memory was too painful for him.

But this was not the first time my dad had told about this secret mission. In my travels to Fairfield I met a man who had grown up with my dad. Without my asking about my dad's former life, he began to relate to me the details of a morning he shared with him at Big Earl's breakfast table. He told me about a day when he and Uncle Earl, as he also called Big Earl, were having breakfast and my dad stopped by. Sitting there at their breakfast table in that home overlooking the land my family would later give their lives to stay on, my dad relayed the most gruesome events of his young life. A memory that he would later hold tight to his chest and let few people in on. This dear older gentleman told me the same harrowing details that Pop shared with me a lifetime later.

But these were not the memories Pop would dwell on. He only wanted to share the good stories with me, not the painful ones. He told me of the good times he had with his buddies onboard the ship. He was a wild one then. He rode a motorcycle, always, and he didn't want to leave it behind when he shipped out of Pensacola, Florida, so he hid his bike on the ship!

Ruthie Shelton collection

IN THE NAVY – "Little Carl" Shelton and his not-quite military issue motorcycle which he smuggled onto his ship while serving in the U.S. Navy during World War II.

"How did you hide your motorcycle onboard a navy ship?" I asked him.

"It was a big ship," he answered. "It had three hanger decks."

Pop raced motorcycles while in the navy. At one race in Pensacola he won an Indian motorcycle. He sold his old bike and brought the Indian onboard. He said maybe fifty people knew about it. He laughed adding, "maybe twenty men rode it on the ship."

Pop was so young when he volunteered for the Navy, his parents had to sign and give their permission for him to join. This is kind of ironic considering he had basically been on his own since his mother Lillie left Dalta, when he was just a little guy. This was something I learned from my research when a distant cousin of mine was able to get Pop's military record and send it to me. I also learned that my grandmother Lillie could not read or write, as she signed the document with her mark, an "X." I also learned that she had already remarried to Roy Miller by the time my dad joined the Navy.

One of Pop's duties when the ship was in port was to transport the navy admirals wherever they needed to go. Pop drove a Jeep when he escorted the officers to shore for meetings. He also drove the Jeep when he *didn't* escort the Admirals to shore. He used the Jeep to carry people to town on liberty. "I wasn't supposed to but I did anyway," he said. That seemed to be the case with my dad in a lot of areas of his life, especially with guns, "I always carried my navy issue .45," he continued, "you never knew what was going to happen." My dad also received several medals for his time in the navy including a purple heart. But he didn't care about those kinds of things. Material possessions of any kind just never really mattered to him. They were just things. It was the people he loved that mattered to him.

There was a live and let live attitude in Fairfield when it came to my dad. He was always a skirt chaser, as was his Uncle Carl before him. Pop always had a girlfriend and one on the side, kind of hidden away, in case the first one didn't work out. (That was all before he met the love of his life, Nell). He would tell me, "It was between this one or that one." It was always his decision. Even after he came to Florida, he had a choice to make, according to him. "It was between your mother and a woman back in Fairfield," I guess my mother won. That's one contest I bet she wished she hadn't been in.

In my dad's younger days he was very free with the gun in Fairfield and no one seemed to mind. He was not physically big like most of the Sheltons, maybe 5 foot 9, slim build. I believe he, and of course Elaine and I, got our shortness from his mother. He was carrying his gun inside his pants waist one day while walking around on the town square in Fairfield. The gun fell inside his pants and slid all the way down to the ground. This happened right in front of a deputy. The deputy reached down and picked up Pop's gun and said, "Here Carl, this gun's too big for you. Let me trade with you," and he took Pop's gun and gave him his. Pop said he thought it was a good trade.

There was a building in Fairfield called the Legion Hall where gambling took place. Pop visited it often. He came out late one night and fell asleep in his car. While sleeping he heard tapping on the window. He ignored it and kept sleeping. Then he heard tapping again. He immediately put his .45 up to the window and as he opened his eyes and looked up he saw it was a deputy. The deputy said, "Carl, it's me, it's so and so. It's okay, it's so and so." Pop couldn't remember the deputy's name. Pop put the gun down and opened the car door. The officer said, "It's alright. We're gonna drive you home." Pop got out of his car and they drove him home.

Not everyone liked my dad's attitude of feeling he was the crown prince of Wayne County. One night at a free show in the park in Fairfield everyone sat around in lawn chairs waiting for it to start, but the show they got was not what they were expecting. My dad, "Little Carl" as he was known, walked right up to the front row of chairs and stood there, looking out across everyone. He stood up straight with his chest puffed out and proclaimed in a very loud voice, "I'm the best damned man here!" Well that was too much for one bystander. He jumped up out of his chair and punched my dad in the face so hard that my dad fell backwards to the ground. Before he could get up the man who hit him was long gone – and stayed out of sight for quite a while!

Ruthie Shelton collection

WHO'S THAT WOMAN – This is one of Ruthie's favorite photographs of her father in what she refers to his "gangster suit." The mystery to her is the identify of the woman taking the photo.

Chapter 14.

Black Charlie Turns

The step I'm now faced with in my writing process is to tell about "Black Charlie" – Charles Bryan Harris. When I wrote an early draft of this chapter summing up his pitiful life and read over it, it was 561 words long. It wasn't until then I realized the animosity my family felt towards this man had passed on to me. Black Charlie was someone I'd never met, never even heard of him, until that day at Pop's bedside when my life forever changed dramatically. He was someone Pop hated. He had a hand in running my family away from their homeland in the early 1950s, but in my opinion, a very small part.

He shot, though never prosecuted, my Aunt Lula and her husband Guy Pennington in 1951. Black Charlie took the final and possibly killing shots to the man my dad was named for, his Uncle Carl, an uncle my dad loved dearly. I don't want to accept or believe that Charlie Harris fired the shots that ended my uncle's life. I don't want him to get what has been called the credit for Big Carl Shelton's death.

So, as you can see, this chapter is difficult for me to write with no bias. I know there are people alive today who feel Charlie Harris had a good side, people he treated well, just as there are those who my uncles treated well and are still alive to tell about it. I guess in reality those treated badly by both sides didn't live to tell their stories. Those are the ones that have been passed down only through the generations or through official records.

But I also realize you can't tell the Shelton story without telling about Black Charlie. Just the same you can't tell the Charlie Harris story without telling about the Shelton boys. Their stories, their lives were so intertwined right from the beginning.

With one very large exception, Big Carl Shelton took the lead, *always*! Black Charlie spent his entire life trying to play catch-up, playing second fiddle to the man *he* wanted to be, Big Carl Shelton.

From the time Charlie started working for Carl as a whiskey runner and spent 10 years in prison in Big Carl's stead, through all those years he allowed himself to be identified as "Black Charlie," although he *hated* that name placed upon him by Big Carl. To the last pull of the trigger riddling Big Carl's already dying body with bullet spray, Black Charlie was *always* second best!

So here goes my take on Black Charlie. Born to John Michael and Talitha Jane Harris, (he was 30 years her senior) on July 26, 1896, Charles Bryan Harris grew up in Pond Creek just down the dirt road from the Shelton family. He played with the Shelton boys and (when he attended) went to church and school with them. For a while during his childhood his parents moved the family to Oklahoma but soon after returned to their lives in Pond Creek. His parents had between them 22 children. He was the youngest child in his family. His sister Cora Mabel who was five years older than him would be his closest sibling growing up and later his ally in life.

Harris left school at 17 years old, after having only progressed to the 6th grade because of being expelled. He was a very small young man physically, with a very large mean streak, a bad temper and because of being the youngest of such a large brood, very, very spoiled. He put on the façade of being a gentlemen, wearing the nicest clothes he could come by, speaking softly and always being polite, at least until he was crossed. Then his very violent temper would show.

He was a skirt chaser from an early age, as were several of the Sheltons. Charlie decided to marry when he was 18 years old, but this didn't change his womanizing ways. His bride would be Lelah J. Smith, a 16-year-old daughter of a farming family in Pond Creek. They married on Valentine's Day, February 14, 1915. Eighteen months later their son Howard was born. That same month Charlie left his young bride and newborn son to pursue what he thought would be a more exciting life in Arizona. She soon filed for a divorce and it was granted.

This was where the true extent of Charlie's violent nature really started to show. On August 15, 1918, police arrested Charlie in Phoenix, Arizona, for knifing an undercover police officer when he and another officer attempted to arrest him. Officers Lew Mickey and Roscoe Broyles had been watching what they believed to be a house of prostitution. When they saw Black Charlie and the resident, Myrtle Thorner Swartz, described as "a notorious woman," enter the house, they followed with the intention of arresting them. After stating their purpose the officers told Black Charlie and Swartz to accompany them to the police station. He would have none of that. He pulled out his knife and stabbed Mickey severely in the side. Harris was still arrested but now faced the added charge of assault.

The judge gave Charlie a two-year sentence but he was paroled early. After being released from prison he apparently headed for Detroit and the booming car plants. He wasn't the only Pond Creek boy up there. His schoolmate and teacher's son Gladstone Keen already worked as a mechanic there. Keen would later return to the farm lands of Wayne County, Illinois, and remain Charlie's ally and alibi in the years to come. By this time Charlie had married Myrtle but it didn't last long. She soon left him for a warmer climate and they soon divorced. In Detroit Charlie helped developed the Shelton's northern route of running liquor, buying booze from across the river in Canada and shipping it down to St. Louis and Southern Illinois.

Big Carl even gave Charles Harris a name that he saw fitting for a two-time double-crosser as Charlie proved to be. "Black Charlie" is what Charles Bryan Harris would be known as for the rest of his life. Some people thought it was said to describe his dark complexion, dark hair and dark eyes, but the Sheltons knew the real reason for the name was to repay him for his back stabbing dealings. He hated the name given him by his number one nemesis, but he still answered to it without complaint!

The time came when the booze was being paid for by counterfeit money, money that belonged to and was *printed for* the Sheltons. Even while warring with the Birger Gang, both gangs used this counterfeit money produced in Southern Illinois off of plates designed by John Mayes of Mt. Vernon. The boys bleached real $1 bills then printed the counterfeit $20 bill on top. It was said to look as good or better than the real thing!

Around 8 or 8:30 p.m. December 12, 1926, just hours after Mayor Joe Adams had been assassinated in West City, Illinois, up at Detroit Black Charlie visited the house of Patrick Walsh to arrange a shipment of Canadian liquor for the following evening. The next day they met up and Charlie used the counterfeit 20s to pay Walsh $1,280 for the liquor. This was when the working relationship between him and the Sheltons soured. You see Charlie had been skimming off the top of the take from the liquor he was running and he thought Big Carl didn't know. Of course Big Carl always knew what was happening. He always knew everything that went on in his organization, sometimes he chose to just let it ride, for a while. Carl had given Charlie just enough rope to hang himself, and that's exactly what he did! The exchange went bad after Walsh tried to deposit the cash, and Black Charlie was arrested for it. He took all the heat for the Sheltons. Of course the Sheltons claimed the counterfeit money was all Black Charlie's doing. Black Charlie spent ten years of his life thinking he was smart enough to dupe Big Carl Shelton into owing him part of the "good life." He was very wrong!

A few weeks later on January 21, 1927, the authorities arrested Black Charlie for dealing with counterfeit money. Four months later on May 11, the judge sentenced him to ten years in Leavenworth. He arrived there two days later.

For three days both my uncles and Harris labored as inmates of the penitentiary. I find it ironic that on May 17, my uncles left for their eventual freedom for a crime they did not commit while Harris would remain in Leavenworth for a crime they actually *did*. It was something he *never* forgot!

On December 15, 1930, Black Charlie earned his parole, but not for long. He violated it and was sent back to Leavenworth to serve time until December 27, 1937. He spent an extra seven months in prison past his original release date because of that violation.

After his release from prison Black Charlie worked for Big Carl again but things were not at all what he expected. He thought he would be treated like a crown prince in the Shelton organization but all he got was bit jobs. Carl knew he couldn't trust Charlie. His true colors had shown when he stole from the Sheltons, but Big Carl wasn't cutting him off completely, not yet. He could still use him, just under closer supervision.

Carl had Charlie work at the traveling skating rink that Aunt Lula ran when it was in Fairfield. In the late winter of 1940, J. C.

"Blackie" Anderson, 35, an oil field worker began dating one of Harris' nieces, Ruby Newman (or Manlove). Sometime in late March or early April Ruby approached Wayne County Sheriff's Deputy Elmo Mugrage "asking for protection and saying that Anderson had beaten her up." On the night of April 24, Anderson and Ruby came to the skating rink on the west side of Fairfield. There around 10:15 p.m. Black Charlie and Anderson got into a fight "over alleged threats voiced by Anderson against Harris' niece."

Charlie stepped in and put Anderson against a wall. As he started to pound him, Anderson pulled out a knife and stabbed Black Charlie in the hip. Big Carl quickly threw Charlie a large caliber gun and unfortunately the gun was quite powerful. He fired two or three shots at Anderson hitting him in the head and chest, fatally wounding him, but he also shot Big Carl!

One of the bullets went through Anderson's body and struck an eyeglass case in Carl's shirt or coat pocket and entered his chest just below his heart. Anderson still clutched the knife in his hand when law enforcement officers arrived. He was found at the edge of the road about 50 feet in front of the skating rink. Not surprisingly no one at the skating rink claimed to have either seen or heard the shooting.[74] What a coincidence that the bullet struck Carl at that exact spot where he had some protection! Personally though, I find it even more of a coincidence that my son is called "J.C." The similarities between the lives then and my life now still amaze me!

---

[74] April 25, 1940. "Carl Shelton, Ex-Gang Chief, Shot in Fight." *Carbondale Free Press* (Carbondale, Ill.). 1; April 25, 1940. "Eyeglasses case Saves Life of Carl Shelton." *The Daily Independent* (Murphysboro, Ill.). 6; and May 29, 1940. "Shelton's Rink Manager Held on Murder bill." *The Daily Independent* (Murphysboro, Ill.). 6.

This story brings back to my mind one slip of the tongue my dad made when I was younger. He loved to roller skate and he was very good at it. He tried to teach me, but it was hopeless, I'm a total klutz. That gene skipped me, but my kids got it. They can balance on

Photographs courtesy of Jimmy Zuber

TRAVELING RINK – That's chief gang henchman Ray Walker in the top photo. He ran the rink for a while. Both photos are believed to have been taken when the rink was set up in Fairfield. It was here that Black Charlie Harris shot J.C. "Blackie" Anderson, and accidently shot Carl Shelton as well.

anything, with or without wheels. If they are on skates, skateboards, snowboards, surfboards, they feel at home, just like Pop.

It was during a trip to a skating rink here in Jacksonville, while skating with my kids, that Pop let it slip that he was "raised in a traveling skating rink." I had a lot of questions about that statement but he, of course, managed to not talk about it.

After the shooting incident involving Harris and Anderson the skating rink went on the road traveling around the Midwest. As one person reported to me some of the music played at the rink was rather risqué for the time and Fairfield residents were not happy with this. So rather than change the music and atmosphere of the rink they simply moved it around.

After Pop's parents, Dalta and Lillie divorced there was no one around to raise him. He spent a lot of his childhood traveling in that skating rink with his Aunt Lula and cousin Jimmy. Pop was paid $1 a day to sweep up after the rink closed at night.

As time went on the strain and distrust between Big Carl Shelton and Black Charlie grew. Harris began to realize that he wasn't going to be rewarded, either with power or financially for his time spent in prison. It all came to a boil when he wanted a piece of land on sale for back taxes and he wanted Big Carl to help him buy it. It sat between two parcels of land already owned by him on one side and Carl on the other. One story says that Carl bought it for himself out from under Harris.

But another story came in the mail to me after I ran an ad asking for the "good Shelton stories." According to the writer, "in the late 1920s or early 1930s, the residents of Fairfield had a problem with Pond Creek flooding parts of the city. They started a petition, and eventually got the matter put on the ballot. Only the people in Fairfield and those who had farms along the upper part of Pond

Creek were allowed to vote; however, the cost of widening this waterway was to be paid only by those farmers along the creek. Of course the largest number of voters were in Fairfield, so the issue passed by a large majority. The farmers along the drainage ditch refused to pay the part of their taxes that funded the project. After some years, the county went through proceedings to have these properties sold for back taxes."

The letter goes on to say that both Carl and Earl attended the sale telling the crowd not to bid. "As they came up for sale, Carl would bid the amount of taxes owed on each property, so all the properties legally belonged to him. At the end of the proceedings, he handed all the papers to his attorney, and instructed him to deed the land back to the farmers who owned each farm."

I don't know if the land Black Charlie wanted to buy fell into that category and Big Carl was returning it to its rightful owner or if, indeed, Big Carl, once again, stiffed Black Charlie, but however it went down, that was *it* for Charlie Harris! When he got out of prison he thought the Shelton boys were going to reward him *greatly* for the ten lost years he endured, but he was wrong, very wrong. Not only did they fail to reward him, they had now become enemies! The Shelton boys had the "use them and lose them" mentality. If they needed someone, they were their best friend for the moment. Once the need had past, they moved on, forgetting whatever had been done for them. Black Charlie learned this the hard way.

Some of the other Pond Creek neighbors were unhappy with the Sheltons also. The more time Big Carl spent in Pond Creek, the more he seemed to think that he owned the *whole* place. He wanted to control everything that happened near his home and, of course, make a few dollars off this endeavor. Big Carl started charging his neighbors a toll of as much as five cents per bushel for them to transport their own crops past his farm! He backed his charge up with threats against the farmers.

Big Carl loved anything that was expensive, even animals. He had purchased nine or ten head of registered Black Angus cattle. They wore chains around their necks with their registration numbers on them. Uncle Carl was very proud of owning them. Pop's cousin, Jimmy Zuber, told me that he had them for less than two weeks when they were stolen by Virgil Vaughan, a relative of sorts to Harris, and another man, by the last name Moore.

Big Carl immediately went looking for them. He found the truck and trailer they had been driven in several counties away, but it was too late. All that remained of Big Carl's prize winning Black Angus cattle were the chains with the registration numbers still on them laying in the floor of the trailer. The beautiful, white faced Black Angus cattle had been taken to be slaughtered. Big Carl was livid! This was more than thievery, this was a slap in the face to him.

Now the search began for the thief. It didn't take long. Big Carl, Little Earl and Ray Walker found Vaughan in a roadhouse. Big Carl, already irate and fuming, accused Vaughan of stealing his cattle. Vaughan picked up a fan and hit Big Carl over the head with it. That was a big mistake! The three of them gave Vaughan a beating he wouldn't forget.

Soon after that Virgil Vaughan and his neighbor Fred Meritt were driving from Fairfield to Albion, about 15 miles away. Meritt lived in Pond Creek and was a neighbor of the Sheltons as well. As they drove a Shelton car came along, shots were fired and at least twelve bullets hit the car. Vaughan's car was wrecked and he suffered serious enough wounds that for the rest of his life he walked with a limp. He spent his later years living as a recluse.

Neighbors say they hardly ever saw him come out of the little two-room house he lived in.

In 1974 John David Moreland of Sangamon State University, now the University of Illinois's Springfield campus, interviewed Meritt. Today his memoir has been transcribed and made available online. "I was riding with [Vaughn] one night going over to Albion," Meritt recalled, "and we was pretty sure it was some of their bunch that shot twelve bullet holes through that car. I never was hit with any bullets but he was hit about three times."

Meritt continued, "We was a ways ahead of them the first shot and they hit the pavement just under the car and the bullet glanced up and hit the bottom of the car somewhere, and they was up pretty close to us and turned in again and I went down in the floorboard; that's how come me not to get hit because they shot a hole right through the back of the seat that I was sitting in and this Vaughan that I was riding with, why he said, 'I think this is our only chance,' and he just turned the car up a bank at the edge of the highway. It just run up there a ways, just about the top of the bank and turned over and right back down on its top. I kicked the glass out and got out to get him out. I was afraid the car would get afire and I reached back in to get a hold of him and he was coming out whenever I reached back in there, I figured there might be somebody following up so I got him up in the cornfield, just at the edge of the road where they couldn't see us, and sure enough there was another car in just a few minutes drove up there and someone looked in the car. And he said, 'There isn't anybody in here.' They made him look a second time but I couldn't tell for sure who it was but I thought I knowed."

Vaughan was technically a step-cousin of sorts, but based on his age, he was more of a nephew of Black Charlie. When Wayne County Sheriff Hal Bradshaw appointed Black Charlie as a *special deputy* to protect Vaughan from the Shelton Gang, it, if nothing else, proves the bias and ineptitude of the law enforcement in those days. The sheriff appointed a *known criminal* as a special deputy. Of course, Sheriff Galligan appointed the Shelton boys special deputies in Williamson County during the Klan War. Thank goodness for modern professional standards.

I met Virgil Vaughan in a nursing home in Fairfield. He was just a frail little man taking a nap when I got there. When he woke up I told him I was Carl Shelton's daughter. I asked him if he remembered my dad Little Carl. He didn't answer me. He was only concerned with having lunch. But then I asked him if he ever worked for Charlie Harris, he got a big smile on his face. He said he wanted to go back to sleep, so I thanked him and left.

Charles Virgil Vaughan died on June 2, 2011, at the Wayfair Nursing Home in Fairfield and was buried at Maple Hill Cemetery. Graveside services were held two days later. There was no visitation. Vaughan was 90 years old.

Chapter 15.
The First Strike

By the mid 1940s Al Capone was no longer in the picture so the working arrangement he and my uncles had was now defunct. No more peace between the two largest and deadliest crime organizations in the Midwest. The Syndicate, or Outfit, as Capone's organization has been called, had grown beyond what even Capone had envisioned. They had merged with some East St. Louis gangsters and were taking over all the racketeering, gambling and liquor distribution in the Midwest. All *except* for the Sheltons!

It was 1947 and both Carl and Earl claimed to be retiring to their farms in Pond Creek. And why not? They each had all the money any normal person could want. They were both in their late 50s and the system they had set up to run the gambling, alcohol and prostitution rings that had given them this freedom to retire, would practically run itself. They each owned hundreds of acres of land in Wayne County. Earl had been spending most of his time farming for a while now. Carl decided it was time for him to do the same, but he wasn't about to let go of any of his business dealings, even to the Syndicate.

The head of the Chicago Outfit was Jake "Greasy Thumb" Guzik. Buster Wortman quickly worked his way to the top by taking over control of gambling joints in East St. Louis. The word went out that the Syndicate bosses wanted the heads of the Shelton gang brought in for negotiation talks. They wanted to "buy out" their gambling and liquor holdings in Illinois. Carl, Earl and Bernie refused. This infuriated the big bosses of the Syndicate. Wortman saw this as an opportunity to gain the power he was hungry for after all those years in Leavenworth. The Sheltons were viewed as country bumpkins and for them to refuse an offer made by the Outfit was a slap in the face to the big city gangsters.

The reward for bringing the Sheltons in was $10,000 for each of them. But no one could get close enough to any of the Shelton gang leaders to hogtie and wrangle them to Chicago. When this was realized the offer changed. Now it was $20,000 a head for each of the main players in the Shelton organization – *dead*!

My uncles knew this hit was out on them. *Everyone* knew. People had even seen Black Charlie meeting with some of the Syndicate and East St. Louis gang members shortly after the shooting and wreck of Virgil Vaughan. These were acquaintances he had made when serving time in Leavenworth. Black Charlie was never big enough, bad enough or brave enough to go up against the Sheltons on his own, but he would jump in as a snitch to let the big boys know where the Sheltons were the most vulnerable, on their own home turf.

Black Charlie saw this as the opportunity he had been waiting for. Now it was his payback time. He knew there were enough people wanting the Sheltons out of Wayne County so there would be no backlash from any violence against them. He also knew the roads taken by the Sheltons coming and going from their farms. So if the Syndicate boys were going to do the job, he would certainly do the informing.

This is the part I just don't understand. My uncles lived in houses with bunkers underneath complete with escape tunnels. They had bodyguards escort them everywhere they went. That was one of my dad's jobs and they *never, never* went anywhere without firepower.

They even ordered special made bullet-proof cars with bullet-proof glass in the windshield and windows, but for some reason not at *"home."*

When Uncle Carl was riding around Pond Creek he felt safe. It seemed he had a false sense of security. This was his home, his old stomping ground. He couldn't possibly imagine that anyone could or would dare try to get to him there. I think he felt a difference in being "Big Carl," rackets king, and just Carl Shelton, farmer. And this was where it showed, but it made no difference to the other gangsters which hat he wore. They wanted him *dead*! For all the brains Big Carl Shelton was reported to have had to run that multimillion dollar organization, sometimes he just wasn't very smart.

October 23, 1947 proved to be a dark day for the Shelton family and the beginning of the war that I was unknowingly born into. Big Carl had farming business to attend to. It was time to bring in the beans, a chore Big Carl took care of every year. It was just another day on the farm to him. He got started early with the farming.

Later that day he had an appointment to meet with a lawyer to draw up his will. Ten days earlier on the 13th Carl and Pearl Vaughn legally married. They had been living together in Peoria, Illinois, for years. Sometimes Big Carl even had another woman living with them, but he loved Pearl, and wanted to make sure she wouldn't be left destitute if something happened to him. With the hits out on him perhaps he had an ominous feeling. Maybe he just knew something was going to happen. Whatever the reason, Uncle Carl was certainly tying up all loose ends in his life.

Uncle Carl always picked up Pop when he went to Pond Creek, *always*. But not this trip. The October 30, 1947, *Wayne County Press* reported that Big Carl, Ray Walker and Little Earl, "drove to the farm early that day in the Shelton truck."

That could be why Uncle Carl didn't pick up my dad, they simply didn't have room for him in the truck. It was a move that ultimately saved Pop's life. They were heading to the fields, "where workers were hastening to gather a large crop of soy beans before rainfall damaged it." The three of them drove to Uncle Roy's house in Pond Creek where Big Carl had left his Jeep. It was the same Jeep Pop always used to drive Carl around Pond Creek imagining that they were safe.

Big Carl had a good sense of intuition. It had kept him alive many times through the years, but this was one occasion he didn't follow his gut feeling and it cost him dearly. He knew in his heart things were about to go badly for him. That's why he finally married his long time girlfriend and that's why he was having his will made out. Still, he didn't pay attention to the warning signs that day.

While in Pond Creek they heard horns blowing in the distance. It was like a code or a warning of some kind. Big Carl, Ray Walker and Little Earl were in Pond Creek the day before and heard similar sounds but nothing happened then. I guess they thought it would be okay that day too. That was the last mistake Big Carl Shelton would ever make, a mistake that proved fatal!

He got in his Jeep and started driving away from Roy's house. As he approached Wagner's Bridge on Beech Bluff Road about four miles in from Highway 15, the gangsters under Buster Wortman's control lay in wait. They hid in the brush beside the road ready for their victim to drive by. Big Carl was wide open as he drove his Jeep through the homeland he loved.

This is the part in the history that varies according to who is telling it. The discrepancies in the stories vary widely but this seems to be the most well known version. As Big Carl drove through the peaceful back country he had called home his entire life, out of nowhere shots rang out. He had been ambushed! His Jeep swerved and Big Carl, already hit several times by bullets, stumbled out. Firing his pearl-handled revolver that he *always* carried with him, he stumbled and fell, head first, into the ditch.

This version of the story says that Ray Walker and Little Earl Shelton drove up to the bridge, stopped the truck, and as they jumped under the bridge for cover, yelled for Big Carl to get down. They never took a single shot at the gunmen because, as the story goes, they did not have their guns with them! Still under the bridge they both reportedly heard Big Carl call out, "Don't shoot me anymore, Charlie. It's me, Carl Shelton. You've killed me already." Then, silence. The shooting stopped. Little Earl and Walker came up out of the ditch to see what was happening.

Little Earl saw the gunmen load someone into the back of their car, at first fearing it was Uncle Carl but later realizing it was one of the shooters' own men that Big Carl had hit with his return fire. The car belonging to Wortman's men took off heading south.

Little Earl and Walker ran to the truck and jumped in to go for help. Suddenly, they saw Charlie Harris running down the road away from them! Walker said Harris turned around and pointed a long gun at them and probably shot because something took out the right front tire of the truck and it ran into the ditch. Black Charlie continued running away. Little Earl and Walker climbed out of the truck and got into Big Carl's Jeep. They left the scene to go for help in Fairfield.

That was the story told about what happened that day, October 23, 1947, in Pond Creek. That story has been repeated countless times over the last 60 some years since my great Uncle Carl was murdered.

It's been told in books, in newspapers, in barbershops, and around kitchen tables. It was told by both Ray Walker and Little Earl Shelton at the coroner's inquest on October 28. The one place it hasn't been told is in Shelton homes, because it is *not* what happened!

The family story has been kept secretive by the closest Shelton family members for many years now. This is the true story of what happened the during the last moments of Big Carl Shelton's life as it was told to me by Pop and other family members.

As the Jeep Uncle Carl was driving approached Wagner's Bridge on Beech Bluff Road, shots rang out from the bushes alongside the road. The Jeep swerved and came to a stop. Big Carl, already hit several times by bullets, jumped out and crouched down behind the Jeep. He was outgunned and outnumbered.

He started returning fire from the pearl handled revolver he always carried. The shooters couldn't take Big Carl down while he was hiding behind the Jeep. The only part of his body now exposed to gunfire were his ankles! The gunmen took aim and fired at the most vulnerable part of him, shooting his ankles out from under him. As Uncle Carl fell he fired off all but one bullet from his gun. He landed head down in the ditch, falling on his revolver.

Before being taken down, Big Carl managed to wound one of the shooters. By this time Black Charlie, who was driving down the road with his niece in the car, heard the shots being fired. He stopped his car and told her to run to safety as he had always trained her to do. I guess the Sheltons weren't the only ones "trained."

Black Charlie ran toward the scene of the shooting, but, as I was told by family, "he was late to the shooting." Whether he knew the shooting would happen that day or not, I don't know. I can't imagine that he would knowingly put his niece in danger by bringing her into the area if he knew before hand, unless it was all part of the plan.

When Black Charlie got to him he saw Big Carl laying there, shot multiple times, probably already dead, head down in the ditch. Black Charlie kicked Big Carl in the foot to see if he was still alive. Whether he was still alive at that moment or not, I don't know and it didn't matter to Black Charlie. There lay the man he had hated for most of his life, finally vulnerable. At this point Black Charlie had what he had wanted for 20 years, Big Carl Shelton in his sights with no way for him to fight back.

Black Charlie opened fire on a dying or already dead man laying head down in a ditch. He sprayed Big Carl with bullets from his machine gun until he was sure his greatest nemesis was dead. He then turned and started running down the road, *away* from the direction Little Earl and Ray Walker were driving.

So the big question so many, including myself have had, why didn't Little Earl and Ray Walker defend Big Carl Shelton? The answer turns out to be very simple. They were too far back up the road to be of any help. Little Earl and Ray Walker *did* have their guns with them, but they didn't get the chance to use them, and because of this, they failed in their main purpose in life – keeping Big Carl Shelton *alive*!

It was two hours before anyone returned to Pond Creek to move Uncle Carl's body. Wayne County Sheriff Hal Bradshaw would not go to the site of the shooting until the Illinois State Police got there. That would be Lt. Ben Blades. Then finally Sheriff Bradshaw took a cab to the scene! To reach the scene of the shooting you have to drive from Fairfield east on Highway 15 to Beech Bluff Road, then drive south for four miles into the Pond Creek bottoms.

When they all returned to the scene, including Big Earl by this time, it was a terrible sight for the family. Big Carl was lying face down in the ditch, his feet towards the top and his head towards the bottom. His face was turned down. Sheriff Bradshaw and Lieutenant Blades wanted him left there until pictures for investigational purposes could be taken. But Big Earl couldn't stand seeing his brother lying there, face down, in a ditch. They picked Uncle Carl up and laid him out flat on the ground.

As they lifted his lifeless body from the ditch, they saw his pearled handled revolver underneath him. Five shots out of the six-shooter had been fired as Big Carl attempted to save his own life or take his attackers out with him. That shows how fast everything happened. Big Carl didn't even have time to get off six shots from the time he was shot out of his Jeep until he fell into the ditch dead.

Big Carl had been hit by at least 17 different bullets from a revolver, a rifle, and a machine gun. He had 25 bullet holes, some in the head, some in the chest, one just below the heart and a dozen across the back and hips. His body was then taken to Nale's Funeral Home in Fairfield. Big Earl put his fingers in the bullet holes so he knew what caliber bullets Big Carl was hit by before the coroner even checked.

Pop had the unenviable task of getting his younger cousin Jimmy out of school and telling him the horrific news, Uncle Carl was dead! The look on Pop's face when Jimmy saw him told a lot. "Uncle Carl's been shot," Pop said as they were walking out of the school. Outside Pop told Jimmy that their uncle was dead.

They rushed over to Nale's Funeral Home where Big Earl and Jimmy's mother, Lula were already there. Lula took the cousins straight in to see their Uncle Carl's bullet ridden body. Jimmy would turn 17 years old the next day. This scene would stay with him for the rest of his life.

"I would never have done that to my kid," Jimmy confided.

We figured Aunt Lula must have had her reasons.

Pearl Vaughn was driven to her father's house. It was only after she was safely there with her family that she revealed to the Sheltons that she and Big Carl had married.

Aunt Lula and Jimmy headed out to her mother Agnes' home to tell her that her boy, her favorite son, was dead. That was a horrible moment. Agnes cried and screamed over and over. "Not my Carl, anybody but my Carl!" No one could console her.

Pop didn't waste time mourning. He wanted to go with the police and pick up Black Charlie. I could see the anger that was still in him when he recalled this day.

"If I had found him, they wouldn't have had to bring him back!"

But the police told him he couldn't go with them. It wouldn't have done any good any way, no one could find Black Charlie by the time they got around to looking for him.

Big Earl was trying to calm the nerves of all the people who were becoming more and more afraid there was going to be an all out gang war right there in Wayne County. He kept telling people that the law would take care of everything. But that was not what he believed. Big Earl bought three special rifles. He gave Pop, Little Earl and Jimmy each a .30 caliber M1 carbine, with one purpose in mind – to kill Black Charlie!

People from all around scurried to the *Wayne County Press* office, as was the custom. Printed only weekly, the paper posted breaking news on their front window. The announcement of Big Carl Shelton's death drew crowds outside the Press office window waiting for the latest updates to be posted.

Others beside members of the Shelton Gang reported seeing Charlie Harris on the road leading down to the ambush site. Gladstone Keen and his wife lived about three-quarters of a mile away. They testified to his presence that day, as did his niece, "Jakie" Bell, who had been in the car with her uncle.

Of the five people who testified that Charlie was at least in the area that day, she is the only one still living at the time of this writing. During my research I've talked to a number of people who have brought up her name. Some encouraged me to talk to her. Others told me to stay away.

After many false starts and dead ends my publisher Jon Musgrave finally tracked down a phone number for her. Should I call, or should I let it rest? My distaste for Black Charlie was even affecting my thoughts about her, a woman I had never met.

"Do you want to make the call, or should I?" he texted.

I told him I would make the call and I did. I told her who I was. She was pleasant, but when I asked about what happened that day she told me she had already told that other researcher, Taylor Pensoneau. She said, several times, "I can't go beyond what's already written."

I thanked her for her time and hung up the phone. For all the nervousness I had thinking about making the call, the actual act of doing so proved to be a letdown. There were no explosions, no hatred, on either of our parts. It was simply the past and the past was over. Since she wouldn't tell me, here's what she told Pensoneau when he was researching her uncle for his book, *Dapper and Deadly: The True Story of Black Charlie Harris.*

"We were on that gravel road not far from the place where Carl was murdered," she told Pensoneau. "We suddenly heard a lot of gunfire. It couldn't have come from very far away, but we weren't close enough to see what was going on. Charlie had always told me to get out of the car and run if shots were fired when we were riding together. So, he yelled to me, 'Remember what I told you. Get out of here and run!'"

"She obeyed instinctively," Pensoneau wrote. She slid out of the car and watched "her uncle drive off in the direction of the shots."

We know Black Charlie didn't fire the first shot at Big Carl but he *did* fire the last. He stood over Big Carl's body laying face down in the ditch and riddled him with machine gun fire. That wasn't a hit, that was hatred! Black Charlie hated Big Carl ever since his time in Leavenworth and he bided his time until he could take his revenge. He didn't care if Big Carl was already dead or not before he shot him, he just wanted to blast him.

Since I learned the truth about my family, I've been asked many times if I know who killed Big Carl Shelton. When I began my research I thought, I hoped, I would be able to find out the answer to that 65-year-old mystery. I have not found any undeniable evidence but I will give my own personal opinion.

The Syndicate and St. Louis mobsters were behind the murder of Big Carl Shelton. I believe it was Buster Wortman specifically. Whether he actually fired the first shots or hired hit men to do his dirty work, he was behind the fatal shots. They were the ones my family went to war with, not Black Charlie, not a man so cowardly that he would machinegun a man already laying dead in a ditch.

The grand jury recommended that Black Charlie be held for investigation but it was too late to hold him, he was long gone. This was the man Sheriff Bradshaw recently appointed as special deputy to protect others against the Sheltons. Looks like he did a pretty good job. After a week of searching for him, Black Charlie was arrested in a bus depot in Tulsa, Oklahoma. He denied having anything to do with Big Carl's murder, though he did admit to being in the area when the shooting happened. He said it was only a coincidence.

After Black Charlie was brought back into custody in Fairfield, Big Earl and Bernie demanded to talk to him. But the Sheriff Bradshaw wouldn't let them near him. After Black Charlie was released on $7,500 bond he went into hiding in Pond Creek, saying he was "afraid of the Sheltons."

The grand jury returned a verdict of no indictment against Black Charlie saying there was not enough evidence to charge him, or *anyone* with Big Carl's murder. The coroner's jury found that Big Carl had been killed "by persons unknown."

About 1 p.m. Friday afternoon the body of her dear son was brought to the home of Agnes Shelton from Nale's Funeral Home. He remained there until about 3 p.m. Sunday laid out in a bronze casket he purchased the year before. Food had been delivered by friends and neighbors. Flowers overwhelmed her modest home and spilled out onto the porch.

The only visible sign that this was not just the death of a well loved neighbor was the fact that the front of the house was patrolled by men carrying machine guns. I was told by one of the visitors that day, "they would stop you on your way inside, if you were okay, they would say go on in."

A steady stream of mourners drove up to Agnes' home. From their Model Ts to limousines they came to give their condolences and say their final good-byes.

Big Carl had made his own funeral arrangements a year before his murder. His casket alone cost $2,500. As in life, in death he spared no expense. It was copper colored and very heavy, made of bronze chrome. It was considered the very latest thing in casket manufacturing and one of the finest made. It was guaranteed moisture proof during the life of the survivors. A heavy grave vault was also used in his burial.

The funeral was held at the First Methodist Church. People lined the street as the procession made its way from Agnes' home into town. It was the largest funeral Fairfield had ever seen. Forty carloads of people drove from the quiet country home where Uncle Carl loved to visit his mama and enjoy a home-cooked meal. This would be the last time he would ever leave that home.

The *Wayne County Press* on October 30 reported, "Estimates of the crowd attending the service and standing on the streets viewing the cortege range from 2,500 to 5,000." I've been told by people who were there it was closer to 5,000.

Lt. Blades of the state police had seven officers in Fairfield that day. There were also four city police officers and the sheriff and his deputies. Many feared a gangland uprising, but in the end all they had to handle was the traffic.

It was a dark, damp afternoon. When the casket was carried into the church it had a transparent cellophane cover over it. "The main auditorium of the First Methodist Church was packed to capacity. It seats around 900. Plus this many folding chairs were placed in the aisles while others were seated in the small Sunday School classrooms on each side. The three balconies were filled and apparently every foot of standing room was occupied."

Reporters came from far and wide to get pictures of the slain gangster and the grieving family. Big Carl's elderly mother, Agnes, was seen being helped down the church steps by family members, she could barely walk because of her grief stricken condition.

Those waiting outside were, as the Press article continues, "taken in to the vestibule of the church at the close of the service to view the remains." This took hours.

So many people were waiting in line to view Big Carl that by the time he was taken to the Maple Hill Cemetery to be buried the sun had set. He was laid to rest next to his father, Benjamin Marsh Shelton, who had died in 1944 from cancer. The cemetery was illuminated by headlights aimed at the gravesite. Hundreds of people stood in the drizzly rain hoping to get a glimpse of history in the making. The final moments in the life and death of Big Carl Shelton.

The same paper that reported on Big Carl's death also ran one of his last business transactions: "Lula Shelton Zuber Pennington sells to Carl R. Shelton the west half of lots 6, 7, and 8 in the David Peer's addition, on the north side of the highway, west of Fairfield. Mr. Shelton had an apartment house under construction there."

Big Carl's widow, Pearl (Vaughan) Shelton, had an especially hard time after his murder. Not only did she have to deal with the grief and normal business matters after the loss of a husband, but she was also afraid for her life, understandably so. She eventually left Fairfield for California where she married John E. Upphoff.

In her later years she moved back to Fairfield. I was shown her grave site in the Koontz Cemetery there in Wayne County with the tombstone that once read, "Pearl Vaughn Shelton." Pearl's new last name of "Upphoff" had been engraved *over* "Shelton" and the spelling of the new surname shortened so it would fit!

Some of the owners of gambling houses that were paying Big Carl for protection now closed for fear of reprisal for having been a Shelton ally. Of the establishments that weren't closed many of the owners gave their control over to the Syndicate. If Big Carl Shelton wasn't safe against them, who was?

A ballad was written recounting the death of my Uncle Carl and subsequent mourning of his mama, Agnes. It was composed by Fred Henson and Big Earl. It was sung by Henson to his own guitar accompaniment. Big Earl was reported to say, "I think it's a wonderful song and a beautiful tribute to my brother."

The song, "The Death of Carl Shelton," still has an audience to this day. I've had many people contact me wanting to know if I had the words to the song. So here they are.

'The Death of Carl Shelton'
As sung by Fred Henson (1948)

Near a little country schoolhouse in the county known as Wayne,
Was down in Pond Creek Bottoms one day a man was slain,
He was riding on the highway to see about some grain
When they shot him from an ambush – Carl Shelton was his name.

Now, little did he know that morn he started out,
These hoodlums would be waiting there along this murder route,
He had no one to warn him, and he feared no earthly harm,
As he drove his Jeep that morning to work down on the farm.

He left his dear old mother in sorrow there alone,
Living down near Merriam in her little country home,
May the angels hover over her – for she hasn't long to stay,
I hope she'll meet her darling in a better world some day.

At the county seat in Fairfield, they could not find the bill,
But we all know that it is not right our fellow man to kill,
They even shot him when he fell and left him there to die,

Some day this mystery will be solved in the courthouse in the sky.

He had four loyal brothers, two sisters and a wife,
To mourn his sad departure the day they took his life,
In Maple Hill they laid him so peacefully at rest,
But his presence, it still lingers, with the ones that knew him best.

He left his dear old mother in sorrow there alone,
Living down near Merriam in her little country home,
May the angels hover over her – for she hasn't long to stay,
And hopes she'll meet her darling in a better world some day.

Photo courtesy of Jimmy Zuber

AT PEACE – Earl Shelton at the Shelton family tombstone in Florida in later years.

Chapter 16.
More Attacks

You would think with Big Carl's murder still unsolved and the $20,000 hits still out on the rest of the major players in the Shelton Gang, the family would have hunkered down, brought in more protection or disappeared. But that wasn't the case, especially with Bernie Shelton. He was stubborn, headstrong, cocky and mean. No one was going to stop him from anything he wanted to do, not if he had anything to do with it. He decided he was going to be the head of the organization now. He lived just outside Peoria, Illinois, and ran his Parkway Tavern on the outskirts of the city, so he thought he could run the business from there. This proved to be his downfall.

It was July 26, 1948, on a hot Midwestern morning and Bernie had driven from his home which he called "Golden Rule Acres" to his tavern on Farmington Road. He had to take care of some business in his office before going to take his car to the garage for some work. Alex Ronitis, one of his bartenders and a old henchman from the gang's earliest days in Herrin during the battles with the Klan, would follow and bring him back to his tavern. The two men started walking out of the tavern together in the wide open with no lookouts or bodyguard around. Bernie thought he was invulnerable.

Ronitis realized he had forgotten his pack of cigarettes and he stepped back inside to get them. This proved to be a lifesaving move on his part, but this left Bernie, who was not a small man, in the open alone. As he walked toward his car a single shot rang out, bringing Bernie Shelton to his knees. As he fell he clung to the bumper of his car. The shot had come from a high powered rifle, from a shooter hiding in the brush at the bottom of a hill behind the tavern.

Bernie pulled himself up and started to stagger back towards the tavern when Ronitis, who had heard the shot and froze temporarily, opened the door. Bernie waved to him to stay there, fearing there would be more shots coming. But there weren't. This was a gangland hit, the second strike in the war against my family. It took just one shot from a .351 caliber Winchester rifle to bring down the Midwest's meanest, toughest gangster, Bernie Shelton!

The shooter and another man, both very well dressed, had driven into St. Joseph's Cemetery on top of a hill near the Parkway Tavern. A path leading down the hill came out behind the tavern. One of the men, high powered rifle in hand, took this path to the bottom of the hill, and waited for his target to appear. It didn't take long. After taking his shot, the shooter ran back up the path, dropping his rifle on the way and got back into the car. The two men took off and made their getaway.

Bernie staggered back inside the tavern and made his way to a barstool. As he sat there, leaning over the bar, it was evident that he was badly wounded He had been shot in the chest. An ambulance was called. When it arrived stubborn Bernie wouldn't get on the stretcher, he decided to walk to the ambulance under his own power. Outside the ambulance he allowed himself to be laid out on a stretcher. From inside the ambulance, he could see a car he thought was following them. Bernie tried to roll off the stretcher onto the floor to get out of the line of fire. The ambulance driver was told to speed up. The car Bernie had seen following them then disappeared.

Taken to St. Francis Hospital he told a nurse to pull off his shoes and pants because he knew he was going to die. One nurse said she knew he must be an important person because of the very large diamond he was wearing. The bullet went in Bernie just below his heart and came out the right side of his body. He had left the home he shared with his wife, the former Genevieve Paulsgrove, at 10 a.m. that morning and by noon he was dead, killed by "person or persons unknown."

Bernie's mother, Agnes, now in her late 80s, had to be told that her youngest son was dead, murdered. Just nine months before she had said goodbye to her beloved son, Carl, now this. How much would prove to be too much for this elderly woman who, just a few years before had buried her husband of 60 years, after being struck with cancer? "Who did it? Was it that dirty dog that killed Carl?" she cried, wanting to know who was destroying her family.

But she wasn't the only one wanting to find out the truth behind the murders. Big Earl told the *Wayne County Press*, "The law could have prevented Bernie's murder if they had solved Carl's killing. I'm through talking. I talked my head off after Carl was killed, but what's the use? We get no protection from the law, so we are trying to watch out for ourselves."[75]

The paper noted, "Bernie, Earl and Ray Walker conducted a private investigation of Carl's murder and reached the conclusion it was the work of St. Louis and Chicago gamblers." In addition it referenced reports by Chicago and St. Louis newspapers noting that "gambling interests had posted a $20,000 reward for anyone who killed either of the Shelton boys or Ray Walker." These stories said that Big Earl and Walker were next on the list. Of course those big city gambling interests – the Syndicate – were using locals who had intimate knowledge of the Sheltons. The family immediately suspected Black Charlie again, but the identity of the second man

---

[75] July 29, 1948. *Wayne County Press* (Fairfield, Ill.). 1.

remained a mystery at least to the public. However, thanks to a Mount Vernon chiropractor with a penchant for history his name can now be revealed. According to Virgil Vaughan whom Gary Atchison interviewed, not only did Charlie fire the fatal shot, his accomplice was fellow Pond Creek farmer Gladstone Keen.[76]

The reports at first said that Bernie would be buried with his family at Maple Hill Cemetery in Fairfield and his funeral would be there also. That's what the family wanted, but Genevieve wanted his funeral and for him to be buried in Peoria, so that was what happened.

Bernie's viewing was like that of Big Carl's. He was in the same type bronze casket and was seen in the front room of his home, Golden Rule Acres, by hundreds of people at the viewing. Afterwards he was taken to the Boland Mortuary for the services. The funeral procession had about 40 cars including the family with his mother Agnes. She was so grief stricken by now, she had to be physically helped to and from the gravesite. At one point she was seen leaning over one end of the casket at the cemetery.

In my mind this image reminds me of my great Uncle Earl's funeral so many years later. Aunt Earline, the grief stricken widow, had *me* take pictures of her kissing her 96-year old deceased husband Earl while he lay in his casket!

Big Earl had a near miss with death years before in Fairfield, and so did my dad. They were at the Farmers Club, the Shelton's gambling establishment across the street from the courthouse in Fairfield. It was a two-story brick building. The downstairs at times

---

[76] Jon Musgrave. March 27, 2012. Notes on phone interview with Gary Atchison, interview of Virgil Vaughan.

held a café and upstairs was a "gentlemen's club," at least that's what it was known as. Law enforcement looked the other way.

On the night of May 24, 1949, a group of men sat on bar stools around a card table playing poker. Big Earl had laid his cards down to say something to friends, when three bullets came flying through the only window that was exposed to the outside. All the other windows had been blacked-out. This window faced the top of a garage that was next door and level with the club's window.

Big Earl was hit by one bullet in the back. Pop was almost hit too, telling me he "heard a bullet whiz by his ear," before he turned and opened fire towards the shooter, emptying his .45 at the window. But it was too late, the shooter had left the way he came, back across the garage roof next door to the Farmers Club and down a ladder that had been left lying against the garage.

Dr. Donald B. Frankel gave Big Earl emergency treatment. The doctor said if the angle in which the bullet entered his body had varied to the slightest degree, it would have killed him instantly. Big Earl was taken to the Deaconess Hospital in Evansville, Indiana. The Fairfield sheriff and police chief followed in Little Earl's car for "security."

For once the family had official protection. Big Earl's injury was serious. Dr. John Visher said it entered Earl's back, passed through his body and broke a front left rib. He felt it would be better to leave the bullet in him rather than continuing to probe for it.

There were guards at his door while Big Earl was in the hospital. The Attorney General of Illinois had requested them. Little Earl also sat in Earl's room to protect him.

Only a few people remained in the club at the time of the shooting, they were about to close and most everyone had gone home. Little Earl said if the gunman had waited just three more minutes they would have been gone. Pop said, "we were warned not to tell reporters who was in the club when the shooting occurred."

Pop was mad, livid, that his uncle had been shot. He said he wanted to get started with the investigation to keep the police from "fouling it up." He stood on the town square and announced, loudly, to everyone in hearing distance, including a deputy sheriff, "I'll take care of this in my own way!" Pop told reporters. "I drew my .45 and fired back, but the varmint got away. But I hope he comes back. I hope he don't leave us alone now."

A big red convertible was reported to have been seen driving away from the scene of the shooting. Pop said when that red convertible was found, "it would have some bullet holes in it!" Black Charlie drove a big red convertible.

Police Chief Hallam was reported to say, "We're sorry it happened, but we're not going to do much about it."

Pop countered, "You can see what's being done. It's easy to see who did it."

Uncle Earl recovered from his injuries but it took a while. The *Wayne County Press* reported on June 23, "Big Earl Shelton was able to be up town Tuesday for a drive, the first time since he was shot in the back several weeks ago. His condition is slowly improving."

He came to town to see the damage of the most recent attack on his kin as well as simply be seen as up and about himself in a show of strength. Although national Prohibition had long been repealed Wayne County itself remained dry, which accounted for the demand for illicit liquor.

Late Saturday night on the 18th just before midnight, the sheriff, state's attorney and Fairfield police conducted a joint raid on a complex of buildings on U.S. Route 45 south of the city. There were at least three buildings in the immediate area, the Roadside Inn which Guy and Lula Pennington operated as a drive-in restaurant, Guy and Lula's living quarters about a 100 feet behind the restaurant and a nearby tavern of sorts operated by Guy's brother Ogie Pennington. The complex also served women as well as liquor, and Guy and Ogie's uncle Taylor Pennington had an ownership stake in it as well.

The authorities arrested four people at the roadhouse and one at the home. They charged four of them with selling intoxicating liquor without a license and the fifth with being an inmate of a house of ill fame. None of the arrestees were the Penningtons.

Between both establishments the authorities also confiscated $2,000 worth of liquor, most of which came from the basement of Ogie's place. The whiskey taken at Ogie's "included some of the finest brand names in the liquor game and there was nearly every size of bottle from half pints, pints to quarts. Much of it still in the original cases, while one large cooling tank was filled with ice cold beer." In addition four large pistols were also taken in the raid.

Once the law enforcement officers had taken the suspects, weapons and alcohol away, the place remained deserted. A few hours later the restaurant exploded in the early hours of Sunday morning waking residents in town. Then, to add insult to injury in a literal sense, someone burned down what was left of the rubble Sunday night.

Sheriff Hal Bradshaw claimed no knowledge of who did either job.

"There could have been 151 people who did it," he jested.

"All I know is we're getting damned tired of it. It can't be reached by law until we know who it is," he added later.

As to the seized liquor Bradshaw said it would be sold to a liquor dealer with the revenue turned over to the county fund. Reporters also questioned my great-grandmother Agnes. She told them she just wished "this shooting would quit. I just can't stand much more. It's just about killed me."[77]

The assaults on the Sheltons kept coming. Even though the law enforcement authorities had bullet shells, fingerprints, the rifle itself in the case of Bernie's murder, even eyewitnesses, the coroner jury's verdict always came back with the finding of murdered "by person or persons unknown."

The attacks against my uncles didn't leave the next generation of nephews out. In the summer of Bernie's murder when Lula's son Jimmy Zuber was just 17 years old he was taking care of normal chores, simply mowing a yard, when he heard a friend yell to him, "Jim, get down!" He ran and hid behind the house. When he paused to take a look he saw Black Charlie standing out front with a rifle.

He told me of another time he thought his number might be up.

"I came home late one night. I pulled into the driveway. I knew something was wrong. Black Charlie came up in his car. He had three guns sticking out of the windows. They didn't shoot," he said.

That was certainly unusual!

Charlie may have thought Jimmy too young to shoot, but he didn't feel that way about Dalta's sons who were in their 20s. On September 9, 1949, late in the night, Little Earl was just pulling up to his house on Elm Street in Fairfield as gunfire erupted from a passing car. The shooter started blasting away with the machine gun when they got near Little Earl's car, first hitting the house, making a straight line across the house before connecting with his car then hitting the house again as they drove away. A bullet grazed Little

---

[77] June 23. 1949. *Wayne County Press* (Fairfield, Ill.). 1; and June 20, 1949. "Bomb and Burn Road House." *Mt. Vernon Register-News* (Mount Vernon, Ill.). 1.

Earl's head knocking him onto the floor of his car. He pulled his gun from his shoulder holster and returned fire as the shooter's car hurried away.

Little Earl's wife Eleanor and their two little daughters were asleep in the house when the shooting started and awoke in terror. Little Earl climbed out of the car from the passenger's side and headed for the front door of the house, leaving a trail of blood behind him. Eleanor ran to the front door and saw her husband covered in blood.

She helped him into the house and got him to the couch. Eleanor called for the older of the girls to go to the phone and call for help. My cousin was so young she had to pull a chair over to be able to reach the phone on the wall. She called her mother's dad and he came straight over.

A doctor called to the house made arrangements for an ambulance to pick Little Earl up. Big Earl rode with them as they transported his nephew to Deaconess Hospital where he had been treated earlier. Little Earl had been pierced by eight bullets. His car had 21 bullet holes in it. There was a line of bullet holes across the front of the house, except for where the car blocked it. Little Earl lived but it was a very traumatic time for his young family. Evansville police stationed a guard at his door in the hospital.

I spoke with a lady who was friends with Little Earl's daughters at the time of the attempted murder. She told me her family heard the shooting that night. Many neighbors came out of their houses but when they learned the target they soon realized it was another attack on the Shelton gang and they all quickly went back inside.

The one-time neighbor said that after that night the windows in Little Earl's house were "blacked-out, covered with something so dark you could not see anything inside." The next thing she knew, her playmates were gone, disappeared. She never saw them again.

The day before this attempt on Little Earl's life he had an opportunity himself to take out Black Charlie Harris. He had a clear shot at Black Charlie but he didn't take the shot. Why didn't he end the terror his family was dealing with?

It was only because Black Charlie had a young girl in the car with him. That was how he stayed safe when he wasn't in hiding from the Sheltons, he kept a young lady with him knowing that the Sheltons would not take the chance of missing him and hitting an innocent girl. It's too bad Black Charlie didn't feel the same way the night he barraged Little Earl's house with bullets while his wife and two little daughters lay sleeping inside.

In May 1950, Big Earl and Little Earl were driving in Pond Creek checking on the progress of some new oil wells that were being drilled. Oil had been discovered in Wayne County and the Sheltons had started their own oil company and were drilling right away. Big Earl had been told that one of his wells was about to come in, so he wanted to go see it. Gunmen opened fire as Big Earl and Little Earl drove onto a bridge over a dredge ditch. A bullet struck Big Earl in the arm and broken glass cut his face near one of his eyes.

Later that spring Little Earl and Dellos Wylie, a former gas station operator in Fairfield before the war, bought a building together about two miles west of Fairfield on Route 45 to use as a garage. Wylie, a father of five, had "been associated for several years with the Shelton family," and like Little Earl, was a World War II veteran in the U.S. Army. He was also an extended relative of sorts as he was first cousin to Guy Pennington's mother.

On June 5, Little Earl had driven Wylie to buy equipment for the garage. They had got back to it and were sitting in Little Earl's car when they heard gunfire erupt from the bushes near them about 75 yards away.

"Earl ducked, shoved Wylie out of the vehicle and followed. They fled into the garage. A second fusillade ripped into the building. Sheriff Elmer Brown said Wylie 'lost his head' and tried to make a run for it, probably to hide behind the building. He was cut down in his tracks."

Wylie took three bullet in his back. After the shooting stopped, Little Earl went out the back door and saw Wylie laying there bleeding badly. Little Earl got him to a nearby house and called for an ambulance. Wylie was in serious condition but he survived.

The sheriff said there were three shooters. He found three different caliber shells, .30 caliber rifle shells, .45 shells and shotgun shells. The shooters definitely planned the attack in advance. In the spot they waited, the weeds were trimmed and they had it camouflaged from the highway. There were also the broken shells from hardboiled eggs in the area, giving evidence that the gunmen had waited some time for their target to arrive, Little Earl.[78]

It wasn't the first time Wylie had been faced with a gun since the war. Two years earlier two men had attempted to hold him up. When one pulled a gun Wylie grabbed for it. The gun discharged in the scuffle. As the men scrambled to get back in the car one of them lost a shoe. Wylie fired at the car but the gun jammed and they got away.[79]

---

[78] June 6, 1950. "Shelton Companion Seriously Wounded." *Mt. Vernon Register-News* (Mount Vernon, Ill.). 1; and June 6, 1950. "Ambush 'Little Earl' Shelton, Partner Shot." *The Daily Register* (Harrisburg, Ill.). 1; and Jon Musgrave. March 8, 2012. Notes on phone interview with Kathryn (Wylie) Moore, daughter of Dellos Wylie.

[79] Sept. 10, 1948. "Lose Gun, Shoe." *Indiana Evening Gazette* (Indiana, Penn.). 14.

The next attack targeted Roy Shelton just two days later. Roy had spent much of his life in prison, not for anything to do with his brothers, but just his own lawbreaking. He had lost his first wife and sons because of this. He wasn't innocent in regard to his brothers' criminal activities though. He was a driver for them at times, running booze and stolen cars between Florida and the Midwest.

One of the most pleasant things I've experienced with writing this book has been meeting my relatives. For a long time I didn't know if my Uncle Roy had any descendents. I couldn't track down his sons to see if they had children, then finally I found her, Uncle Roy's granddaughter. She has grown children and grandchildren and it was such a delight, not only to talk to her, but to know that Roy Shelton's line will continue.

In March 1949, Roy had been in a car accident in St. Louis which resulted in a fractured jaw and a broken leg. Police were so sure his injuries were the result of gang warfare they posted a 24-hour guard at Barnes Hospital where he had been taken. After a week the police were convinced that his injuries were just the result of wreck.

"Police Chief Jeremiah O'Connell yesterday removed the police guard at Barnes Hospital where former convict Roy Shelton is a patient. O'Connell said he believed the 63-year-old member of the old Shelton gang might have been attacked by gangsters, but received assurance from Illinois authorities that he was injured in an auto accident near Springfield, Illinois. Shelton's two brothers, Carl and Bernie, were slain from ambush and their assailants are still at large."

And at the writing of this book, they still are, or at least would be if they hadn't since died![80]

Roy had remarried and was living in one of Big Earl's houses in Pond Creek. On June 7, 1950, he was farming Big Earl's land, about a mile from the spot where Big Carl was murdered. It was about 7:45 in the morning and he was on a tractor plowing a field. Frank McKibben, a farmhand, was working in the same field. The Sheltons and McKibbens had always been close. The McKibbens had a big family, maybe ten children. They lived in one of the Shelton's houses. Mrs. McKibbens and Agnes Shelton would go to church together in Big Earl's car as Agnes didn't drive. After Ben died, Uncle Earl would send one of the McKibbens' girls to Agnes' home to stay with her so she didn't have to be alone.

As Roy plowed the field, gun shots rang out from behind brush next to the field. Five shots were fired, two of them hitting him. A bullet to his spine killed Roy instantly, but that wasn't the end of it. What happened next was gruesome. When he fell from the tractor seat the disc and harrow ran over him, mangling his body. McKibben ran to turn off the tractor before it ran over Roy again but the gunman then targeted him. He still managed to get the tractor turned off before he had to take cover behind it. The shooter fled.

A man who was in a nearby field driving cattle ran over to the scene. McKibben sent him to get Big Earl. Later, Big Earl sent Dorothy, Pop's first wife, to pick up McKibben from the field and drive him home.

Another time of breaking the news to my poor great-grandmother that a son has been murdered! Another funeral to plan

---

[80] March 14, 1949. "Former Gangster Roy Shelton Hurt in Auto Accident." *The Daily Register* (Harrisburg, Ill.). 1; and March 15, 1949. "St. Louis Police Remove Guard Over Ex-Convict." *The Edwardsville Intelligencer* (Edwardsville, Ill.). 2.

and attend. The service was held in the Dixon and Crippin Funeral Home in Fairfield. About 250 people were able to get inside the chapel out of the more than one thousand that came. The rest had to wait outside. Again the procession moved from the funeral home to Maple Hill Cemetery. He was buried next to his father Ben and Big Carl. This was the third deadly strike against my family! Another Shelton murdered by "person or persons unknown."

Agnes was helped to Roy's casket and she patted it with her hand and said, "Good-bye, Roy."

Just hours after the funeral arsonists set fire to the building where Little Earl and Wiley had been ambushed earlier in the week. It was one of the few unsuccessful attempts on the family. The man who had sold the station to them drove by and noticed the flames. He called the fire department and they put it out before it could cause serious damage.[81]

Big Earl and Big Carl had not let my grandfather Dalta be a part of the gang. I was told it was because he "wasn't smart enough." Well, I think the next event in the Sheltons' lives proves he, of all people, was smart enough, at least, smart enough to stay alive. About two months after Roy's murder Dalta left! He packed up, sold his farm on the Cisne Curve and moved to Jacksonville, Florida. This proved to be advantageous to the family later because he bought land. Big Earl already owned quite a bit of property in Florida.

When my sister Elaine and I were in Fairfield researching we drove out to see Dalta's house. It must have been a beautiful home in its day. It is a two-story brick house with a nice front porch though it had gotten pretty dilapidated by the time we saw it. The kitchen

---

[81] June 12, 1950. "What Next? Shelton Family Wonders After Fire Attempt." *Sheboygan Press* (Sheboygan, Wis.). 26.

cabinets had fallen down and there was a hole you could see daylight through in the roof. And there were dead ("How dead?" Elaine asked) deflated raccoons in the living room.

We did a little sleuthing to find out about the house. We were told no one was able to live there after Dalta left because they would be *shot*!

The sheriff strongly suggested to Big Earl that the rest of the Shelton family leave Pond Creek and Fairfield for good, but Big Earl wouldn't hear of it. He was *not* leaving his land and his home. Little Earl echoed his sentiments. Even Agnes when asked if the family was leaving got mad and said no. She wasn't leaving her home and her children would not even think about leaving their mother.

But what happened next started to change their minds. Big Earl and his wife Earline lived in a beautiful home in Pond Creek. They were very proud of their $35,000 home and the craftsmanship that went into the building of it. Appropriately called "Hill Top Farm" they built their home on top of a hill that overlooked their beautiful land. Thick, heavy drapes hanging from a runner, covered the big picture window in the living room. The closets in the bedrooms were all built with cedar paneling. "We put in everything we could think of," Big Earl explained. They even had a bunker built under the house for safety in case they had to escape from an attack. But they couldn't escape from this next attack. It came in the middle of the night and caught them completely unaware.

In November 1950, Big Earl and Aunt Earline awoke to the sound of glass shattering in the living room. It was three in the morning when they jumped out of bed and ran into the living room and found the beautiful picture window broken and a can laying on the floor. But that was only the beginning. Aunt Earline called the sheriff. Then, what they least expected! The tin can was actually a *bomb*! And the bomb exploded! The explosion blew both back into other rooms. It injured neither one of them but the fire burned the house to the ground. The flames spread so fast they barely got out with their lives. They had no hope of saving their home.

Uncle Earl and Aunt Earline stayed with Aunt Lula while they made arrangements to leave Fairfield. They couldn't leave immediately because Uncle Earl had to pick up my dad, Little Carl, in Indianapolis, Indiana. They had to wait on him to get out of jail. When he was released, they picked him up and took off for, as everyone thought, parts unknown. They told no one where they were going or when they were leaving. They just *left*!

Photo courtesy of Jimmy Zuber

BETTER TIMES – The Shelton family around 1940 includes Roy, Carl, Earl, Dalta and Bernie in the back row, and Lula, Ben, Agnes and Hazel in the front.

Chapter 17.

Final Straw

The month of June 1951 became a very eventful one in the Sheltons' lives. The Shelton boys' youngest sister, Lula and her husband, Guy Pennington, lived in Fairfield. As they drove home from the grocery store they met a car blocking the road at NW 9th and Water Streets. A barrage of gunfire hit their windshield. Lula came out of the car and stumbled to a patch of weeds by the ditch where she dropped to the ground. She saw a man she later identified to police as Charlie Harris standing over her with his machine gun. He was about to finish the job when the gun jammed. She screamed and cried, "Don't shoot me. I've never done anything to you." He hit the machine gun and fired at her again. Lula said Harris was laughing as he fired and shouted, "Now you are going to get some of the stuff your brothers got."[82]

Just at that second Guy's brother Ogie drove up. Black Charlie saw Guy running toward his brother's car and he took aim at him. Then his machine-gun jammed again. Black Charlie jumped back in his car and took off. Aunt Lula was hit with six bullets and four struck Guy. They were both taken to Fairfield Memorial Hospital and listed in serious condition. They both told the police who pointblank shot them – Charlie Harris. But, as was always the case, Black Charlie got away free and clear.

---

[82] June 29, 1951. "Black Charlie Harris Is Free On Bond." *Mt. Vernon Register-News* (Mount Vernon, Ill.). 1.

A few hours later the *Wayne County Press* had another murder headline posted on the front window. Louis Sons had been found murdered at Ogie's tavern south of town! Though listed as a Fairfield "laborer," and other papers described him as a farmer, he actually worked for the Sheltons in the oil field services company.

Ogie Pennington "worked" as a bootlegger and gambler and spoke with a speech impediment. He had just witnessed his brother and sister-in-law gunned down in the street and had gone to his tavern for a drink. When he arrived about noon, H. A. Wall, his bartender was there. Shortly thereafter Louis Sons arrived and Wall left. Ogie said he and Sons drank whiskey together for about 30 or 40 minutes. Then he told Sons he was going to close up and Sons asked if he could stay on a while and offered to close up for Ogie. They were such good friends that Ogie agreed.

After Ogie left to drive into Fairfield, Paul Hodges of Albion, arrived at the tavern wanting to buy some beer. He bought a half case of beer from Sons and left. Ogie said he had driven around in Fairfield for about 30 minutes scared to death about his brother's shooting and then returned to the tavern. When he went in he found Sons shot to death!

Ogie left the tavern and drove back to town and told a gas station attendant to notify police of Sons' murder. He said he then went to get his wife and mother, Maud (Wylie) Pennington, to take them back to the tavern but they refused to go. They had a beautiful home and his mother ran a boarding house. Jimmy Zuber told me a story about her. "Ogie's mother was real nice. I was at the boarding house once and she heard me say I liked potato soup. She was hard of hearing and she thought I said I liked tomato soup. She made me a big bowl of tomato soup and I ate it all. I hated tomato soup."

Wall said he returned to the tavern about 2:15 p.m. and found Sons' body. Wall sent word for the police to come. By the time Ogie had returned to the tavern the police were already there. When he got out of the car he was arrested for driving while drunk. Police Chief Otis Hallam told the Associated Press he was operating on the theory Sons might have been killed because he witnessed the shooting of Lula and Guy, but others suggested the killer might have mistaken Sons for Ogie, who had witnessed the earlier shooting.[83]

Ogie told the coroner's jury, "I don't know who could have done this, I just figured they were here trying to kill me. I don't have a better friend than Sons." The next night Ogie's three-room shack of a tavern burned to the ground. The question of who did it was never even asked, certainly it was never answered.[84]

The grand jury returned an indictment against Ogie Pennington on July 31, 1951, charging him with the murder of Louis Sons. Sheriff Elmer Brown served the warrant issued the next day. Soon taken into custody Pennington posted a $10,000 bond paid by himself, Anthony Pennington and Maud Smith, and was released.

In a time that it was extremely unhealthy to be a Shelton, to be married to a Shelton, or be connected with the Sheltons in any way, the law seemed to overlook one very important factor in Sons' murder. He worked for the Sheltons! It never came up that he had been an oil well worker for the family. This, along with the fact that he was alone in the business of one of the key witnesses to Lula and Guy being gunned down, should have put a whole different slant on the investigation, but it didn't.

---

[83] June 29, 1951. "Black Charlie Harris Is Free On Bond." *Mt. Vernon Register-News* (Mount Vernon, Ill.). 1.

[84] July 5, 1951. *Wayne County Press* (Fairfield, Ill.). 1.

Louis Sons' funeral attracted a crowd similar to that of the Shelton boys who were recently murdered in Wayne County. The funeral procession to the cemetery was more than a mile long.

There was a change of venue in the case against Ogie Pennington. The trial was moved from Wayne County, Illinois, to Marion County with a trial date set for September 8. A case of perjury also hung over Pennington's head and his bond for this was set at $2,500. He had lied under oath to a grand jury claiming he did not illegally engage in the sale of alcoholic beverages.

At the same time, Guy and Ogie's uncle, Taylor Pennington, also faced murder charges in Johnson County, for the holdup and murder of a wealthy Kansas City, Missouri, magazine publisher at a Vienna motel on January 17. As newspapers covered each trial they often provided updates on the other, and almost always mentioned their connections to the Sheltons.

At the trial the evidence against Ogie Pennington was deemed to be circumstantial. A circuit court jury consisting of ten men and two women took four and a half hours and found him innocent.

After several weeks in the hospital Lula and Guy were improving but had not recovered enough to be discharged. That didn't matter to Big Earl. He said it was time for the rest of the family to leave Fairfield, and they did!

I spoke to the niece of a lady who was in Lula's hospital room the night the family left Fairfield. She told me how her Aunt Sal related the events.

"Aunt Sal told me the Sheltons were very nice people. She had known Agnes for years. They went to church together. She told me, 'two Shelton men came in the hospital room late at night, and told me to turn my head towards the wall and cover it with a pillow so I don't hear anything what's happening. I did what I was asked.' The next morning when the nurses discovered Lula was gone they asked Aunt Sal what had happened. She told them, 'I sleep pretty sound, so I don't know.' Aunt Sal told me Lula was taken out from the hospital room through the window by two Shelton men."

Jimmy drove his grandmother Agnes, and his mother and step-father, Lula and Guy, to Mt. Vernon, Illinois, to his girlfriend Barbara's apartment. There they met up with Little Earl. The last of the Sheltons would now head south to their new lives in Jacksonville, Florida.

One structure was still left standing on Big Earl's homestead, but not for long. In June 1951, Big Earl's barn at Hill Top Acres was bombed and burned. It was 9 p.m. when the barn, described as a "large, modern structure" worth about $7,000 dollars, turned to ash and embers.

Ray Walker's wife Louise had more than enough of the gangland violence. She had gone through a horrifying incident in 1944 when she and Ray were living in Herrin, Illinois. One day she was riding in the car with Ray. Out of nowhere Buster Wortman and Blackie Armes ambushed them. Ray took two shots in the arm. Louise was not physically injured. In March of 1952 their house on Big Earl's property burned down thanks to an arsonist. He and Louise were still living there at the time of the fire. It was still completely furnished and was said to be worth about $18,000. After the arsonist set the fire the back door was left open to create a draft so the fire would spread faster. The fire and smoke certainly caught the attention of the locals. A group of people stood and watched it burn.

That was the final straw for Louise Walker. Ray agreed to a divorce and he drove her to her sister Mildred Jolly's home in Michigan. Louise soon remarried to Earl J. Crake. She lived out her life far away from the gangland shootings and arson fires that once drove her from her home. She later died in Flint, Michigan, on April 7, 1983, survived by her husband.

After his Louise left him Ray tried to move on. He went to Peoria thinking he could step right into Bernie Shelton's shoes, in more than one way. He tried to take over the business end of the organization. He did a dismal job of that. He was a hit man and that's all he ever was. He also took up with Bernie's widow Genevieve. With the Capone Syndicate taking over or destroying all of the Shelton business endeavors Ray and Genevieve moved out west to Reno, Nevada, where they appeared in the 1953 city directory under assumed names, Mr. and Mrs. Ray Paulsgrove. He worked as a carpenter and she operated April Beauty Shop, the same name she would use in later years when they returned to Illinois.[85] They lived together for many years and finally got officially married on July 28, 1971, in Elko, Nevada.[86]

This is one question I've been asked by many people: "What happened to Ray Walker?" I talked to Ray's daughter from his first marriage to Faye Perry. She knew who her dad was but he didn't raise her, maybe for her safety. She had a few letters between her parents and knew her mom sent her dad pictures of her. She said that she only met Genevieve, or "Jen" as Ray called her, once in 1955 at her Grandma Walker's funeral. Genevieve died in 1974. After her death Ray moved to Cordova, Illinois. Later, Ray's daughter and her husband spent the weekend in Cordova with him.

"I enjoyed my time with Ray very much," she told me. He also came to her home to visit for a weekend shortly before he died.

---

[85] 1953 City Directory of Reno, Nevada. U.S. City Directories, 1821-1989 (Beta). Ancestry.com.

[86] Nevada, Marriage Index, 1956-2005. Ancestry.com.

In his later years, Ray Walker became a recluse. His daughter told me his only companion was his dog Molly. One day Molly didn't come out of the basement and Ray, fearing she was dead, couldn't go down and get her. He called Genevieve's sister and brother-in-law to come help get her out of the basement. With his beloved Molly gone, now Ray was completely alone. He made plans to go visit his daughter, but before he could go, he fell and broke his hip. He was taken to the hospital where he died five days later on August 25, 1981.

SHELTON GANG – Carl, Earl and Bernie Shelton's 1927 mug shots followed Ray Walker (1935), Blackie Armes (1926), Max Pulliam (1929) and Charlie Harris (1932). All are Leavenworth mugshots except Walker's which was from Menard.

Chapter 18.

65 Years Later

At the writing of this book it has been 65 years since Big Carl Shelton was gunned down while driving through his homeland of Pond Creek. Many books have been written about the "Shelton Gang." From their rise to fame to their fall into infamy, the media has been there. Newspaper and magazine articles written about them over the years have not just entertained and informed but have changed lives.

My mother's life was definitely changed because she read a magazine article and found out who her husband really was. She went from having a normal life to living a day to day existence in terror knowing she was the wife of a gangster.

My life has certainly changed since Pop told me about his past. I began to read everything I could find, which was a lot, with the Shelton name on it. I was finally able to see pictures of my family. This meant the most to me. To see what the generations before me looked like and where I got certain traits from.

My sister Elaine, whom I had only met once, received the newspaper with Pop's picture on it. After seeing his picture and realizing his age, she contacted me. She made the decision they should meet. Since that meeting Elaine and I have been part of each other's lives.

All these books, newspaper and magazine articles show the interest then and now in the Shelton Gang. The interest escalated after the murder of Big Carl Shelton. This was a murder that was never solved. As far as I can see there was no attempt made by either the police or FBI to establish who shot him.

The murders of Bernie Shelton and Roy Shelton shortly followed. No effort to find out who sent one deadly bullet into each of these men was ever made.

There were also assaults on the lives of several Shelton family members. Even when the assailants were specifically identified no efforts were made to apprehend them.

Many people still want to know who was behind the murders. While I've been working on this book, I've been asked a lot of questions. But the one that is *always* asked *first* is, "Who shot Big Carl Shelton?" I guess it's assumed that if we had the answer to that question it would also lead us to find out who killed his brothers, Bernie and Roy. I have found multiple websites dedicated to those who want to put together the clues and figure out who was behind the murders.

To me, it is just as, if not even more important, to find out who murdered my grandmother, Lillie. Her death was not even called a murder. It was listed as "cause undetermined." I think this is the worst offense of all, to not even dignify this little old lady by telling the truth about her end.

There was evidence from each murder. Witnesses of sights and sounds, a rifle left at the scene, bullet casings left behind. Evidence that was swept under the rug. The death of my grandmother was never even questioned. She was murdered, in her bed in a nursing home before 7 a.m. Someone had to have seen or heard something!

But people were afraid to speak up and in the cases of my uncles some were glad to see them gone. The Sheltons had ruled and run Wayne County for years. Big Carl even made the farmers pay a tax to truck their crops past his land. No one dared to oppose the

Sheltons over the years. Many people now saw the murders as an end to their tyranny.

But not everyone felt that way. Some people felt it was a blatant miscarriage of justice that no one was ever prosecuted for the murders. Others are just interested in the mystery of it all. The "who done it" factor that has become so popular keeps people trying to guess.

When taking journalism in school you are first taught to ask the who, what, when, where, why and how of every situation. We have most of those questions covered.

Big Carl Shelton was shot on October 23, 1947, in Wayne County, Illinois, ambushed and assassinated on the way to his bean field. Newspaper accounts and FBI files help explain the why.

In the 1930s when Monroe "Blackie" Armes and Frank "Buster" Wortman did time at Leavenworth, and later Alcatraz (in the case of Armes), they met and became friends with a number of other gangsters from St. Louis and Chicago including Egan's Rats member Frank "Cotton" Eppelsheimer who was doing time for a 1923 mail robbery at Edwardsville, Illinois; Elmer Dowling, another north St. Louis gangster; and Murray "The Camel" Humphreys of the Chicago mob. Alcatraz released Armes in 1940 and Wortman got out the following year.

Once out they started back looking at opportunities in the MetroEast region, or the Illinois side of the St. Louis region. With the Sheltons not physically present in the MetroEast region as they had been in the 1930s they found an opportunity to exploit.

"[Wortman] and Blackie Armes, however, are stated to have been peeved because of the small automobiles given them, and later Wortman turned against the Sheltons and, together with the Armes brothers, joined the ranks of the St. Louis Eganites."[87] Eventually they settled into "jobs as St. Louis area agents for Jake 'Greasy Thumb' Guzik," the head of Capone's Syndicate, as crime reporter Carl Baldwin later summarized. "At least 26 'spot' murders which have been perpetrated in downstate Illinois and in Missouri, can be traced to events created by this illicit agency," he added.[88]

FBI files indicate a third former member of the Shelton Gang switched as well, but went back to the Sheltons. The feds blacked out the name of the third man, but then mentioned that Armes later shot and seriously wounded the man. I can't prove, but I believe that was Ray Walker. The timing fits with what we know, but it's also possible that Walker was acting as a spy for my uncles. It's never been clear to me how Ray's brother Harry took part in the Klan's raids, even the one against Uncle Earl, and then was able to switch sides to the Sheltons unless he was already working with my uncles in some capacity during the raids.

The FBI dates the official split between Armes and Wortman with my uncles to 1942. When it comes to Black Charlie it's important to remember that after he shot J. C. Anderson in 1940 (and my uncle Carl), he left Fairfield and Wayne County for a time. His Leavenworth records include a letter from the DuPont corporation in 1941 after he applied for a job at their explosives plant in Indiana. It's not clear if he got the job, but by 1942 he was working at the Illinois

---

[87] Special Committee to Investigate Organized Crime in Interstate Commerce. 1951. *Investigation of Organized Crime in Interstate Commerce. Part 4-A, Missouri.* Washington, D.C.: United States Government Printing Office. 817-818.

[88] Shelton and Birger Gang Wars file. Carl Baldwin Collection. University Archives. Southern Illinois University-Edwardsville.

Ordnance Plant in Williamson County when he registered for the draft that year.[89]

Herrin had quieted down tremendously after the bloodshed of the 1920s, but it still had the Armes' brothers. Blackie's older brother Floyd, also known as "Jardown" from his days with the gang in the 1920s, had since found God after getting out of the state penitentiary on a statutory rape charge. His life changed after a prayer meeting at his in-law's house. By the late 1930s or early '40s he was teaching Sunday School to the youth at Herrin's First Baptist Church across the street from the Masonic Temple where he had taken part in the deadly Election Day Riot shootout that left six men dead.[90]

Floyd was out of the gang's activities and by the 1944 had moved out to Arizona for his pulmonary health, but Blackie and Jardown weren't the only Armes brothers in Herrin. Roy, who went by Tony, and Ray, known as Lefty, had just been young kids during the Klan and gang wars of the 1920s. By the '40s they had grown from juvenile delinquents to dangerous gangsters following more in Blackie's footsteps than Jardown's.

The FBI thought the expansion of the Egan Gang elements into Southern Illinois caused the former Shelton henchmen to rethink their position. They re-aligned themselves again, this time directly with the Chicago Syndicate that had developed out of Capone's organization. Armes and Wortman became lieutenants of the group. When Ray Walker either returned to the Sheltons, or if the blacked

---

89 Charles B. Harris (#27702) Inmate File. Leavenworth Penitentiary Records. National Archives. Kansas City, Mo.; and World War II Draft Registration Cards, 1942. Ancestry.com.

90 Jon Musgrave. May 2, 2012. Notes on phone interview with Pamela (Armes) Goodwin, daughter of Floyd "Jardown" Armes; and Jon Musgrave. May 11, 2012. "Bootlegging gangster to Sunday school teacher." *The Daily Register* (Harrisburg, Ill.) 1.

out name wasn't him, finally rejected any suggestion to switch sides Armes and Wortman tried to gun him down on the streets of Herrin in 1944.

Later on that year on December 13, Thomas Propes, owner of the White Castle tavern on the outskirts of Herrin shot and killed Blackie Armes after the two had argued in Propes' tavern. The two had been shooting craps on the bar when Propes left to go into a back room to get his gun. Ironically the last person Armes talked to that night was the waitress who worked for Propes. She had been Armes' brief first wife in 1926. Propes returned to the bar, shot Armes, and was then promptly shot by Armes' men.

It's not clear why he shot Armes or how he thought he would survive Armes' friends, but he did it anyway. Like Pop, Propes had served in the Navy earlier in the war. Unlike Pop, he also served as a special deputy sheriff in Williamson County.[91] He was also a brother-in-law to Earl Walker, Herrin's counterpart to Bernie Shelton in terms of controlling the local coin-operated machine racket. Whatever Propes' reasons, he had previously been good friends with Armes, the local FBI agents who followed the gang's actions reported back that the Shelton Gang took credit for the killing.[92] Newspaper accounts reported that Armes' younger brother Lefty and their first cousin Roy Daugherty arrived at the tavern just after the shooting. Both would play a role in the future.

---

[91] Tommy Man Propes."[n.d., c. 1942] Recruit Identification Card. "Blackie" Armes folder. Local History Room. Herrin City Library; and Sheriff William Shannon. July 22, 1944. Tom Propes Special Deputy Sheriff card. "Blackie" Armes folder. Local History Room. Herrin City Library.

[92] Jon Musgrave. March 29, 2011. Notes on phone interview with Loudene (Propes) Strunk, daughter of Thomas Propes. Propes married Earl Walker's sister Mae. Earl's branch of the Walker family is not believed to be closely related to Ray and Harry Walker's side.

Daugherty's older brother Hobson had been "close friends" with the Sheltons and likely an active member of the gang in the 1920s. On Dec. 12, 1927, he joined Ray Walker in a drive-by shooting that targeted Herrin Police Chief John Stamm and his assistant Elmer McCormack, the brother of Mayor Marshall McCormack, while they stood along the side of Herrin City Hall.[93] Roy was born around 1911 and was too young to participate in the activities of the gang during Prohibition, but by the 1940s was a close associate of his cousins. He didn't have a police record connecting him with the mob, but authorities couldn't find any "indication that he was steadily employed." Instead law enforcement officials recognized him as a professional gambler.[94]

By February 1945 the territory controlled by my uncles had shrunk considerably. Wortman and his Elmer "Dutch" Dowling's territory extended from Peoria, Illinois, on the north to Evansville, Indiana, on the east and Paducah, Kentucky, on the south.[95] Previously when Wortman was leading the Syndicate's operations out of East St. Louis they had focused on operating a racing new service which provided them with a stake in the illegal gambling dollars being spent by returning servicemen. This didn't compete directly with my uncles, but with World War II over and the

---

[93] Jan. 11, 1928. "Attempted to Murder Herrin Police; Indict 2." *Carbondale Free Press* (Carbondale, Ill.). 1. The newspaper named Hobson as Hobart, but criminal records spell the name as Hobson.

[94] April 23, 1947. "Herrin Man Found Shot To Death At Crab Orchard Lake." *The Free Press* (Carbondale, Ill.). 1, 4; April 24, 1947. "Inquest Testimony Gives No Light on Daugherty Shooting." *The Free Press* (Carbondale, Ill.) 1, 5; and April 24, 1947. "Herrin Murder Probe Is Continuing Today." *Dixon Evening Telegraph* (Dixon, Ill.). 16.

[95] Special Committee to Investigate Organized Crime in Interstate Commerce. 1951. *Investigation of Organized Crime in Interstate Commerce. Part 4-A, Missouri.* Washington, D.C.: United States Government Printing Office. 817.

economy expanding the Syndicate decided it was time to expand. They began taking over the growing number of casinos popping up throughout downstate Illinois. This was when the competition between my uncles and Chicago turned deadly. The first shots didn't take place in East St. Louis, Fairfield or Herrin, but at Peoria.

As Baldwin put it, "in 1946 Capone gunmen continued hacking away at the arms of the octopus that was the Shelton gang, getting closer and closer to the Sheltons themselves. The battleground was switched to Peoria, Ill., and between February and November the names of Frank Kraemer, tavern owner; Joel Nybert, "strong arm" man, and Philip Stumpf, were added to the slaughter. All were Shelton associates."

By the spring of 1947, it was a Wortman and Armes ally found dead, shot to death near Crab Orchard Lake southwest of Herrin – Roy Daugherty, Armes' cousin who had been present for Blackie's death three years earlier and questioned as a suspect in Propes' death. For a professional gambler it was a professional hit. He had likely been picked up in Herrin and beaten before taken to the lake. There his killers got him out of the car and shot him first in the back of the head before firing two more times. Once dead they dragged him down to the edge of the lake where fishermen found him the next morning.[96] He had been arrested for questioning along with

---

[96] April 23, 1947. "Herrin Man Found Shot To Death At Crab Orchard Lake." *The Free Press* (Carbondale, Ill.). 1, 4; April 24, 1947. "Inquest Testimony Gives No Light on Daugherty Shooting." *The Free Press* (Carbondale, Ill.) 1, 5; and April 24, 1947. "Herrin Murder Probe Is Continuing Today." *Dixon Evening Telegraph* (Dixon, Ill.). 16.

Blackie Armes in the 1932 killing of Oliver Alden Moore by the Sheltons.[97]

After Blackie Armes died in 1944 his brothers seemed to take over the Syndicate's influence in Herrin and headquartered on the second floor of a downtown building two doors down from the old European Hotel, the site of the deadly Young-Thomas shootout two decades earlier.[98] When Daugherty's wife couldn't find her husband the night of April 27, she immediately went and found Tony Armes and his wife. They searched together, but didn't find him.

When Carl was killed newspapers often referred to the fight as between East St. Louis and Fairfield-based gangsters, but every once in a while Herrin would be named. Newspaper accounts noted that Tony Armes' car had been seen in the area of Pond Creek. Years later Virgil Vaughan confirmed to a Mt. Vernon researcher that he talked with Armes and the second shooter after the ambush at the house where they were staying across the road from him. Vaughan wouldn't identify the other shooter because he was might have still been living.[99]

"Underworld gossip names three St. Louis hoodlums as the men who poured 20 shots into Shelton on a country road near Fairfield. State's Atty. Mills said today he believes that is the true story. And at least two of the three gunmen are understood to be intimately connected with the Chicago syndicate," reported the *Chicago Daily Tribune* at the time. Besides Ray Walker and Little Earl's testimony

---

[97] Special Committee to Investigate Organized Crime in Interstate Commerce. 1951. *Investigation of Organized Crime in Interstate Commerce. Part 4-A, Missouri.* Washington, D.C.: United States Government Printing Office. 815, 817.

[98] Jon Musgrave. Oct. 7, 2011. Notes on phone interview with Peter Russo, grandson of Jake and Lena Cacciabaudo.

[99] Jon Musgrave. March 27, 2012. Notes on phone interview with Gary Atchison, interviewer of Virgil Vaughan.

investigators had finally independently linked Harris to the crime after the testimony of Russell Slatterly, a St. Louis pipefitter, who "told St. Louis police he had accompanied Harris last month on a visit to the Plaza Amusement corporation, a juke box distributing concern in the Missouri city. Among its stockholders are several notorious hoodlums." Those hoodlums were headed by Wortman.[100]

There was other evidence that Black Charlie and Tony Armes had a close relationship. Five months later Harris would be arrested again in suspicion for a payroll robbery in Illinois. With him would be Armes and Dale Stamper, an East St. Louis tavern keeper. The three were cleared when the victims did not recognize them. Both Harris and Armes were armed at the time of their arrest.[101]

Armes got his just desserts three months after Roy Shelton's murder when he was gunned down outside the Green Lantern tavern on the north side of Herrin. It was an ambush and authorities questioned Black Charlie in connection with it, but whether it was a mob hit, someone trying to clean up a loose end, or as his relatives have heard, a revenge attack for sleeping with the sheriff's wife, no one knows.[102]

By the time the U.S. Senate's Special Committee to Investigate Organized Crime in Interstate Commerce started poking into Wortman's dealings they gave a good idea of what his, and to some extent, my uncles' businesses were like.

---

[100] Frank Winge. Nov. 1, 1947. "Fear Gang Reprisal on Shelton Suspect." *Chicago Daily Tribune*. 1, 4.

[101] Mar. 10, 1948. "Three Picked Up in Holdup Probe." *The Edwardsville Intelligencer* (Edwardsville, Ill.). 1.

[102] Sept. 25, 1950. "'Bloody Herrin' Gang Warfare Breaks Out Again; Roy Armes of Shelton Gang is Slain." *The Dixon Telegraph* (Dixon, Illinois). 1.

"The local controlling gang today consists of the core of the surviving members of the Egan gang, some former Sheltonites, and a few former Cuckoo gangsters.

The extermination of the Sheltons has left this one group in the control that the Sheltons formerly enjoyed in this area. The newly formed group in gang control operate both legitimate and illegitimate businesses. Among their legitimate enterprises are the operation of a truck line, coin-operated amusement-machine businesses, a loan agency, a string of race horses, taverns, restaurants, and night clubs, and the like. Their known illegitimate activities include handbook operations, gambling casinos, and number rackets."

The gang murders of the 1920s the committee found focused on control of the illegal liquor business. By the 1930s the focus shifted to controlling labor unions. "Shortly after 1940 the pattern of murders changed and it became obvious to law-enforcement officials that the murders from then on constituted a studied plan of assassinations to control all large-scale commercial gambling and vice from a line from Peoria south and even across the Ohio River and also in the St. Louis area."[103]

---

[103] Special Committee to Investigate Organized Crime in Interstate Commerce. 1951. *Investigation of Organized Crime in Interstate Commerce. Part 4-A, Missouri.* Washington, D.C.: United States Government Printing Office. 818.

Chapter 19.
Settled in Florida

After my family left Fairfield in 1951 they headed for Jacksonville, Florida. Some members of the Shelton family already had a firm foothold here. I can certainly understand why they chose to make Jacksonville their new home. Besides the fact that they owed the Florida coastline for most of their ill gotten income, it's just an incredibly beautiful place to live. Although some members of the Shelton Gang had been murdered, the family business would go on. Maybe not exactly as before in the Midwest. But there was still a family that had to be provided for, and for some members of the family, it had to be quite lavishly.

It didn't take long for at least some members of the family to start up business as usual again. Big Earl began purchasing a few small motels in southern Georgia. These motel were not advertised for the travel weary family customers. The rooms came furnished with only two items – a bed and a prostitute. And since he already had experience with slicking the palms of governors, it would be no problem to keep these motels up and running without interference from the local law enforcement.

There was also the land that was owned by the Shelton brothers' that were assassinated. There were no worries about the widows keeping any land, or for that matter, oil rights that belonged to their deceased husbands. As long as the widows wanted to stay healthy and alive that is. The ownership to any properties, on or below the ground was signed over, without question, to the *blood* Sheltons.

Big Carl owned property in Jacksonville which after his death Pearl Vaughn, his widow, deeded over to Hazel McDonald, the Shelton brothers' sister. The same was true with Bernie. He, also owned property here. After his death, his widow Genevieve, also, deeded property to Hazel.

Big Earl owned a beautiful two-story house in Riverside, a historic part of Jacksonville that is still beautiful to ride through and admire the houses and parks. He bought the house next door also and broke it up into four apartments. His favorite real estate investment was called simply, "The Farm." It was a small house on a few acres here in Jacksonville that he sometimes rented out. This was also where Uncle Earl kept his livestock – horses, cows, goats, anything that made him feel like he was still that farm boy back home in Pond Creek.

My grandfather Dalta already owned land here too. He allowed Little Earl, Jimmy, and Pop to put mobile homes on his land to live in until they bought houses. Dalta was a skirt chaser all through his life. He had so many girlfriends and wives, neither Pop nor Jimmy could count them all. Jimmy told me he spent the night at Dalta's house in Cisne, Illinois, when he was young. Dalta had a lady friend there when Jimmy went to bed. When he got up the next morning there was a different woman making Dalta breakfast. One of my cousins told me that Dalta's last wife, although they were already divorced, was with him through his final struggle with cancer. Dalta died December 22, 1960, here in Jacksonville, Florida. He was too sick by the time I was born to have met me so there are no pictures of me with my grandfather.

Aunt Hazel had been living in Jacksonville for years. The first property in her name dated back to the early 1930s. Big Carl bought an orange grove that he gave her to run. This worked out well for her and her husband Guy. Although when they were in the Midwest he worked for the Shelton boys. One of his jobs was to fix the slot machines – in the Shelton's favor of course. I was told this by Pop and Jimmy. When the family first came to Florida, Lula and Guy were still recovering from being ambushed and shot multiple times, so Hazel had Lula and Guy stay with her until they were well enough to get their own place.

It was extremely hard on my great-grandmother Agnes, leaving her little home in the country, the place where she had so many memories of her long marriage and life with her husband of over sixty years, Benjamin Marsh Shelton. In her little country home she never had all the new conveniences available to her now living with her son or daughter in Jacksonville. Some of these really confused her. One story told by family members had to do with Agnes watching television. She was living with her youngest daughter Lula, here in Jacksonville at the time. When she was going to watch a show on TV Agnes would put on her favorite dress, lipstick and perfume. She had to be at her best because she thought the people in the television could see her too. I think she was just ahead of her time. I wonder what she would think of today's technology.

Family members tried to trade off who had Agnes live with them. For a while Uncle Earl and Aunt Earline wouldn't tell where they lived because they didn't want her staying with them. She could be a little difficult at times. Most of the time she lived with her baby girl Lula.

The person I've enjoyed learning about the most during this journey has been my great-grandmother Agnes. I think Agnes was a tough woman who had endured more than her share of grief in her long life. I could see a lot of myself in her. She cooked huge meals and fed everyone, including regularly feeding strangers. This is something I've been known to do. She never learned to cook less after her large family was gone. Same here, I'm still cooking for an army though all my kids are grown. She loved her kids coming in her kitchen, sitting around the table, eating and talking, that's what she lived for. I'm glad I in some small way got to know her.

Agnes (Gaither) Shelton died in 1957, here in Jacksonville. She was not taken back to Fairfield to be buried next to her lifelong love, Ben. Instead, for reasons of safety, she was buried here in Jacksonville.

Pop became a carpenter after fleeing to Florida. He hung acoustical ceilings and worked mostly out of town. I only knew of him working in Atlanta and Miami, but after he told me about his past, I found out he also worked in the islands. I have to wonder what kind of acoustical ceiling work could take him from Jacksonville to the Bahamas. The union he worked for did not send their men out of the states. I also know of times as a kid when there were large amounts of cash in Pop's car. I really don't know when his "past" life really became his past.

Little Earl started driving a truck after moving his family to Florida. He was on the road a lot. Pop told me that when his brother would get back in town after a long road trip, his wife, Eleanor, would say, "Let's go for a drive." All Little Earl wanted to do was put his feet up and *not* drive, but he knew life had been hard on his family in their early days, especially on his wife, so he would take her for a drive. He and Eleanor raised a happy and loving family. Little Earl died here in Jacksonville in December 1998.

Over the years, whenever the family got together at Big Earl's house, everyone would sit around in the living room and talk. Then Big Earl and Pop would wander off into another room followed by

Little Earl or Jimmy, then the other one, until only the "non-Shelton Gang" members of the family were left sitting in the living room.

Things were not totally peaceful in their newfound home. One morning in 1970 Aunt Lula walked outside to pick up the newspaper when she was hit by gunfire. The wounds weren't life-threatening and the assailant never found. I could not determine if the assault was a backlash from the old Fairfield days or just the repercussions from my aunt's party girl lifestyle.

Though in exile, the family still owned hundreds of acres of prime farmland and oil rights back in Illinois. In April 1951, Earline and Lula went back to Fairfield for the sale of family property. Black Charlie bought Uncle Earl's land! I know he had the right to buy it, but to me, that was a slap in the face. Black Charlie Harris owning Shelton land! He paid with a personal check through another person. He didn't even have the guts to pay for it himself. While visiting Fairfield, Aunt Earline was asked by reporters where the family had gone, she wouldn't say. Always classy, she held her head high and replied, "I'm happy where I am."

Big Earl leased some of his 900-acre Hill Top Farm to other farmers. But this didn't work out for him or the renters. The land that was leased to others could not safely be farmed. Anyone who tried to farm land that was still owned by the Sheltons was shot!

On June 6, 1951, E. Hillary O'Daniel, Jr. (called Little Hill) was shot when farming the land he leased from Big Earl. The first two shots were warnings but the third hit O'Daniel in the arm. Two friends who were there talking to him when the shooting began took cover behind a truck. They took him to Fairfield hospital. A lesson hard learned for O'Daniel, no one would be able to farm Shelton land!

Even after the last of Ben Shelton's family left Wayne County the attacks against them continued. On December 2, 1951, Ben and Agnes' home, the original Shelton family homestead burned to the ground. Agnes did not take the news well. It was a six room, frame house with a nice front porch, valued at about $15,000. This was not a small amount of money in 1951. But no matter the monetary value, it was her home. Maybe she had hoped someday she could return. Now she knew that couldn't happen.

Three months later the arsonist struck again. On March 28, 1952, neighbors of Big Earl's farm once again woke up to the sight of roaring fires as a one-and-a-half story frame tenant house and Ray Walker's one-story concrete house both went up in flames. The buildings had previously been shot up. Although no one in the family doubted that Harris was the one behind it, Sheriff Elmer Brown, denied any accounts connecting Harris to the crime.

"Brown has denied receiving any official reports that Charles (Blackie) Harris – an avowed enemy of the Sheltons – has been seen patrolling the farm area recently armed with a sub-machine gun. He also denied rumors that 'Black Charlie' has been riding horseback over remote regions of the farm, with rifle and pistol handy."

All he would say, "someone doesn't intend for Big Earl to farm that land, but I don't know who it is."[104]

The family oil wells could not be properly maintained either. Anyone who went on Shelton land to do work for the Sheltons or tried to lease Shelton land was shot! Still, they managed to keep the checks coming.

---

[104] March 28, 1952. "Shelton Farm Home Burned at Fairfield." *Greensburg Daily News* (Greensburg, Ind.). 1.

Even after what was left of my family fled for Florida and Uncle Earl was established and doing well financially here, he wanted to return to his land. I didn't understand his desire to return home when I first learned about my family. I thought, "Uncle Earl had a great life in Florida, why would he want to leave and put himself at risk just to go back to a piece of land." Then I spent time in the Midwest, in Fairfield, in Pond Creek, even roaming around this land he loved so much on foot. I now understand. Uncle Earl wanted to go home! He even requested special protection from the governor to return and farm his land! Being he had so many public officials in his hip pocket for so many years, right up to and including more than one governor, he really thought he could get federal protection. It wasn't given and he did not return for many years.

By July 1952 with all the Sheltons long gone from Wayne County, Big Earl still owned one piece of property in Fairfield. It was the well-known Farmers Club across the street from the courthouse. He was in the process of selling it to Randall Quindry, a local attorney. Quindry had sent Big Earl the papers to sign to finish the deal but he had not returned them yet. At 1:15 a.m., July 15, on a hot Tuesday morning, an explosion rocked downtown Fairfield so loud it woke half the town and was felt and heard three miles away. The blast damaged at least a dozen buildings on the town square. It even blew out windows in the courthouse. Officials estimated the damage toll to be as much as $100,000.

Roger and Betty Nicks had just remodeled the downstairs of my uncle's building to open Betty's East End Café. They had saved ten months for the project and had just opened the restaurant the day before. In the hours following the blast which left "a hole the size of a wash tub" in the concrete floor by the front door, Roger pledged to reporters that he would re-open. "I'm going to live out the term of the lease if they let me live that long." While he told reporters he could not identify the "they" in his comment, his wife certainly thought she knew the culprits. She didn't tell the press, but according to one of her daughters, she did tell the White House when she tried to call the president. "She was a fire-eater I tell you. She got upset and everybody knew it," recalled her daughter Deborah.[105]

Neither Roger or Betty had immediate connections to Wayne County, so they probably didn't realize they had become the latest casualty of a long-running war. They had come from Mt. Vernon in next door Jefferson County. Roger, just 27, was returning to civilian life after nine years in the U.S. Air Force where he had originally lied about his age in order to enlist at the age of 17 during the first year of the war. While stationed at March Air Base in California his wife Betty worked as a waitress at Lee and Leon's Cafe out in nearby Riverside. After a brief time in Mt. Vernon, Illinois, they soon moved over to Fairfield to open their dream. Despite their plans to reopen Roger and Betty used their heads and followed the example of my relatives. They moved, except rather than the sunny shores of Florida they headed for the high plains of Montana where they operated a series of cafes and restaurants in Miles and later Baker.[106]

It seemed someone didn't want Big Earl Shelton to make a penny and they didn't care who they hurt.

---

[105] July 15, 1952. "Bombs Earl Shelton's Building." *Mt. Vernon Register-News* (Mount Vernon, Ill.). 1-2; Jon Musgrave. Feb. 9, 2013. Notes on phone interviews with Vivian Blake and Deborah Jean Hickey Singer, daughters of Roger and Betty Nicks.

[106] U.S. World War II Army Enlistment Records, 1938-1946. Ancestry.com; 1951 Riverside (California) City Directory. Los Angeles: Los Angeles Directory Co. Ancestry.com. U.S. City Directories, 1821-1989 (Beta) [database on-line]. Ancestry.com; and Social Security Death Index. Ancestry.com.

This was the end of everything "Shelton" in Wayne County, Illinois, except the mineral rights that my uncles had been smart enough to hold onto when they sold their land. Many of the oil rights had been put in their mother Agnes' name to keep them hidden.

Guy Pennington's brother, Ogie, moved to Florida as well. Jimmy arranged for him to have a job as an inspector where he was working. He eventually returned to Illinois and died in 1959. Ogie was a good worker, not the case with Jimmy's stepfather Guy. He was said to be "allergic to work." After Lula and Guy divorced, Jimmy drove Guy back to the Midwest where he started over in Louisville, Illinois, finally working, running a pool hall. His time back in the Midwest wasn't without trouble. He allegedly shot off a man's finger in a fight after he left the Curve Inn tavern east of Ashley with the man's stepmother in 1961.[107]

Seven months later he decided to re-locate again re-opening Frank's Pool Room down in Murphysboro, the county seat of Jackson County where he and Lula had married in 1947 before all the shootings started. A vacant house he owned in Murphysboro burned mysteriously in '69. Investigators found a pail and a kerosene-soaked mop at the site. The bank later repossessed the property. He ended up in Danville, Illinois, where he died on St. Patrick's Day 1971.[108] According to family lore he was poisoned. A

---

[107] Dec. 5, 1961. "Mt. V. Man Shot In Hand; Hold 2 For Questioning." *Mt. Vernon Register-News* (Mount Vernon, Ill.). 1; and Dec. 6, 1961. "Pleads Innocent in Shooting Case." *Mt. Vernon Register-News* (Mount Vernon, Ill.). 2.

[108] July 15, 1962. "Pool Room is Reopened." *Southern Illinoisan* (Carbondale, Ill.). 14; Jan. 2, 1947. "Marriage Licenses." *The Daily Independent* (Murphysboro, Ill.). 1; July 28, 1969. "Fire cause investigated." *Southern Illinoisan* (Carbondale, Ill.). 2; Sept. 5, 1969. "Legal Notices." *Southern Illinoisan* (Carbondale, Ill.). 18; and Social Security Death Index. Ancestry.com.

relative of his told me, "there was enough strychnine in him to kill ten mules!"

Big Earl didn't, couldn't, stay away from his home forever! He made his first trip back to Fairfield, Illinois, when he was 88 years old. The headline in the *Wayne County Press* read, "'Big Earl' Drops By His Old Hometown." I think the first sentence of the article said it all, "A dapper 'Big Earl' Shelton appeared on the public square in Fairfield about 3 p.m. Monday!" Of course his first stop, in true Shelton fashion, was the sheriff's office, then to the Press office. The article continued, "Stepping along like a boy of 16, 'Big Earl' paid a visit to the sheriff's office at the courthouse… and then made his way along Main street to the Press office in spite of numerous delays caused by friendly handshakes and conversations with old friends." Uncle Earl expressed his feelings of finally being back home again, "These people are so wonderful… and I enjoy visiting with them… they haven't forgotten me." There were also some depressing moments during his and Aunt Earline's visit home. "During the brief time he was in Fairfield he drove out by the big, beautiful hill-top farm south of Merriam that once was his. 'It made me feel sad,'" was his response."

Big Earl Shelton lived to be 96 years old. But his last years were not happy ones. He suffered from deteriorating health and his mind was affected badly. At times he thought he was reliving his past in the war days of Fairfield. He would even hide under the tables because of his anxiety and fear of someone trying to kill him. He died October 8, 1986, down here in Jacksonville. He's buried at Riverside Memorial Park with most of the Shelton family. Aunt Earline died in 1994 and was buried next to her husband.

Aunt Lula had died a few years before Earl on June 2, 1980, here in Jacksonville. I remember saying to Pop, "at least she's out of pain now." Pop's reply, "I know, but she still didn't want to die." She had suffered from throat cancer. Her last husband Harry Barger had her buried in Riverside Memorial Park as well.

Aunt Hazel lived the longest. She had remarried and resided many years in St. Petersburg, Florida. She died Hazel Zahn in 1997, and is buried there on the Gulf Coast.

My dad's cousin Jimmy Zuber married Barbara Wallace on September 5, 1951, in Mt. Vernon, Illinois. They had a small ceremony at the church across the street from Barbara's apartment. Rain was pouring down as about fifteen people, some members of Barbara's family and a few close friends, ran to the church. Jimmy and Barbara raised a family and have had a wonderful life here in Florida. At the writing of this book they have already celebrated their 60th wedding anniversary.

Photo courtesy of Jimmy Zuber

POP'S COUSIN – Jimmy Zuber was the youngest of the Shelton nephews associated with his uncles in the Shelton Gang and is the last of his generation of the family still living.

James and I recently spent a lovely day with Jimmy and Barbara at their home on a beautiful lake here in Florida. We try to visit as often as we can. Jimmy is Pop's cousin, and the last link I have to Pop. He is the last surviving family member of that generation. We talked about the book I'm writing. Barbara said, "Ruthie, you're living your dream." I guess I am.

Chapter 20.
Finally Finding Elaine

The newspaper article in the *Wayne County Press* detailing Pop's return visit to Fairfield had far reaching effects. My sister Elaine was sent a copy. We had only ever met once. Now there's a story in itself, Elaine and my meeting for the first time. After the day I found her picture as a child she had never been mentioned to me again and of course I never asked any questions.

It was 18 years before I learned of Pop's past. James and I were at Pop's house and James went over to a cabinet to get a tool. He saw a cigar box open with pictures in it. Pop always kept his most important things in cigar boxes. Pictures, titles, money, his WWII medals, if it mattered to Pop, it went in a cigar box!

"I just found a bunch of pictures of you, but they couldn't be of you because they are too old, you weren't born yet," James came in and said to me.

"Oh, that's my sister," I said without a second thought.

"But, you don't have a sister," James looked so puzzled, we had been married for years and had three children together and he didn't know I had a sister. I guess I had been trained a little too well.

James was from a big family, he was the baby of ten brothers and sisters, born in Tennessee, and they were very close.

"Wouldn't you like to meet her sometime?" he asked.

That got my brain going, "Who is she, where is she, what kind of life does she have, would *she* want to meet *me*?" All these questions poured into my head at once. I'm so thankful that James put the idea into my head of meeting her. Until that moment any thoughts of Elaine stayed locked safely away in that little "box" in my head where I kept all my "Shelton secrets."

But it was the 1980s and you couldn't just go online to find someone like you can today. "Let's talk to Pop," I said. Now I was excited about the thought of meeting my sister. I had no way of knowing the wall I was about to hit, head on and hard!

I approached Pop with the idea of us seeing Elaine. I cannot begin to describe the pained look on his face just at the mention of her name. I had no clue what had gone on or why she was not part of his life but I knew this was the most heartbreaking thing he had ever faced. He told me staunchly he did not know where she lived, where she had grown up or anything about her family. I was *not* to try to locate her or find out anything about her.

I could not possibly know that Pop had sacrificed and spent his whole life with one goal – to keep both Elaine and me safe, even if it meant he could not have her in his life. And he was not about to change anything that could put all our lives in jeopardy.

Of course I didn't know any of his reasons. I was determined to find her, to set straight whatever had happened to hurt Pop so badly, to make her part of our family, and I had to do it without hurting Pop anymore. So I had to look for her without him knowing.

I first talked to Aunt Earline. She was no help at all. She told me the same thing Pop told me. No one knew where Elaine was, and there was no way to contact her. It all started to sound like a broken record. Apparently she was as well hidden as I had always been.

I tried to track down where the pictures were taken, I looked closely at the cars to see what year it was and I finally was able to get her last name from a relative. James and I traveled a lot then so I checked phone books all over the country. Still I found nothing. She appeared to be almost as invisible as I was.

I finally told Aunt Earline that I was going to hire a private investigator to find Elaine. She was my sister and I felt I had a right to meet her. At this point Aunt Earline gave me Elaine's maternal grandmother's phone number. I called her.

I almost choked on the words, "I'm Carl Shelton's daughter," not knowing what kind of reaction I would get. But my worries were unfounded. I've never spoken to a kinder, sweeter, more understanding person. She was Elaine's favorite person in the world. I always wished I had a grandmother like her.

She told me Elaine was 11 years older than me, she was married and had children. She said Elaine knew that I existed but that was all she knew about me. I told her that I just wanted to be able to get in touch with Elaine. Eventually I was able to send Elaine a letter. I could not understand why everyone was so secretive, all I wanted was to meet my sister!

Elaine received my letter and, as she told me later, "I stood there staring at it. Why did I write a letter to myself?"

Our handwriting is so much alike she thought it was hers, and we even used the same stationary! She finally wrote me back, very cautiously, not knowing what I wanted or if the request to see her was really from me. Then we talked a few times. Finally I asked if we could meet. This was very difficult for her because she was raised, as she said, "With a box in her head to put all the Shelton stuff in. It all had to be kept secret."

Even the fact that she was a Shelton had to be kept a complete secret for her safety. Elaine's mother even had her name legally changed when she was five years old.

We lived hundreds of miles apart, but that didn't matter to me. She agreed on a time and place. I was never more nervous in my life. Here I was about to meet my sister, the little girl in the picture I found so many years before.

We were so much alike it was scary. We looked somewhat alike, about the same size, same hair, but our personalities and actions told that we were sisters. James said we even walked alike. We both lived a great part of our lives in the country with horses and dogs. And we both named our daughters "Jenny," which is really crazy when you consider the bombing of the Shady Rest was committed by the Sheltons from a "Curtiss Jenny!"

We were together 10 minutes when, as Elaine puts it, "I knew you didn't have a clue about Carl's past. That's why I didn't have any further contact with you until the article came out." We visited for a little while, talked about our husbands, our kids, our lives, where we lived, and what we did. She told Missi when she should "hit your daddy up for ice cream money." It worked.

At one point we were sitting on a swing, talking, and my son, J.C., came running around the corner.

"It was like seeing Carl all over again," Elaine said when she looked up and saw him.

There were a lot of tears that day.

We spent a few – very priceless in my opinion – hours together, then we hugged goodbye. Elaine got in her pick-up truck and drove home. She told her husband all about meeting me.

"That girl doesn't have a clue about Carl's past and it's not my place to tell her," she told her husband.

I could tell it wasn't the right time for us to know each other. I didn't know why that was the case but I was just thankful to have met my sister. We spoke a couple of times after our meeting, but we didn't stay in touch. I always felt that when the time was right she would call me and we would get to know each other. So now this war that had kept me and my sister from knowing each other when I was a child would continue to keep us apart! We were about to lose another 20 years that we could have been together.

Shortly after my family and Pop visited Fairfield Elaine received the *Wayne County Press* in the mail. She opened it and saw the picture of James, Krystin, Pop and me on the front page.

"Why is Jill's picture on the front page of the *Wayne County Press*?" she first thought.

Her youngest daughter, Jill, and my youngest daughter, Krystin, look just alike and act even more alike. Then she saw the rest of the picture with Pop. She read the article and now she knew he had finally told me the truth about our family, everything that she couldn't tell me 20 years before.

A few days later she was driving home and thought to herself how that elderly man, her biological father, might need closure. He might need to know that his daughter was okay, that she was raised by loving parents and that she had a good life. She wanted to let him know that she had no hard feelings towards him.

Without a thought of herself or what it would mean to her life she called me. She asked if he would want to see her, if he was physically and emotionally up to it. I answered with a resounding, "Yes and come on."

I immediately went to see Pop. I told him Elaine had called and she wanted to see him.

"When does she get here?" was his immediate response. He had tears in his eyes as I told him she was practically on her way.

Elaine and her husband flew to Florida a few days later. We are alike on this count too, when we decide to do something, we do it...

now! James and I met them and we drove out to Pop's place together. Pop and Elaine met each other with outreached arms, hugs and tears.

Elaine assured Pop that he had no explanations to make to her. She was raised in Fairfield, Illinois, and knew about the Shelton Gang. "I know everything there is to know about the Sheltons," she told Pop so he wouldn't have to worry about telling her like he had to tell me. He could just enjoy getting to know his daughter.

Now Pop's life had truly come full circle. Not only had he shared with me all the truth about his past life but now he had his daughter Elaine back in his life. Even though, as we found out, she was never "completely" out of his life. He had so many pictures of her growing up. Through all the secrecy and covering up any trails of where he was, Pop managed to stay connected to Elaine's life. She never knew he had pictures of her and sent presents to her through other people. She never knew he loved her all those years.

Elaine and I were raised as total polar opposites. She was raised in a small town by very respectable, law abiding parents. She was not allowed to shoot guns or play cards. I taught her to play poker later during one of Pop's hospital stays. Of course Pop won.

Nell said we acted like teenagers together. I guess we were making up for lost time. That same time in the hospital, Nell told us to go eat something in the cafeteria. We did not want hospital food so we were going to sneak out to the car and go to a restaurant to eat. When Pop didn't feel well he didn't like us to get too far out of sight so we didn't want him to know we were leaving the hospital.

When we got downstairs we realized we didn't have the car keys. We couldn't go back for them because Pop and Nell would know we were leaving the hospital. So here we were, two adult women, running down this four-lane road during rush hour traffic, crossing it, to be able to eat and get back before they realized what we had done. We got back to the room, out of breath.

"That sure took you girls a long time," Pop said.

"Yeah, sorry," we said, still out of breath, not daring to look at each other for fear of bursting into laughter. I'm sure Nell knew we had slipped out.

Whenever we wanted to do something we knew Pop wouldn't like, maybe going to the beach before we went to see him, I'd always say, "You tell him, he won't get mad at you. You're new!"

It was true, whatever Elaine told him, he would say, "That's okay. You girls do what you want."

Pop was diagnosed with kidney cancer in January 2009, and the doctors said he only had a few weeks to live. He was under hospice care at his home. They are doctors and nurses who come to the home to care for the terminally ill. They put Pop a hospital bed in his living room so he could watch the animals and birds out the front window.

I called Elaine with the news. She asked me when I wanted her to come, I said as soon as she could. She flew in the next day. That's just how she is, if someone in her family needs her, she is there for them.

My favorite memory of Pop and Elaine happened when she got here that next day. I picked her up at the airport and we drove out to Pop's house. He was laying in the hospital bed in the living room and his nurse was standing by him. We opened the door and Elaine walked in first. Pop's face lit up, as it always did when he saw her.

He said to his nurse, "This is my daughter, Elaine! She just flew in to see me. Oh, and that's my daughter, Ruthie," pointing to me.

That nurse had a look on her face like she had been slapped!

I put my arm around Elaine.

"Yes, she's the princess," I said, as we both burst into laughter; and we laughed until we cried.

Pop loved me and I have no doubts about that. We were always there for each other. But Elaine was "new" so he was always excited to talk to her or see her. He had missed out on her entire life and now, here she was. I will always be thankful for that!

Through the few visits and the many phone conversations they had, Pop felt like Elaine had become a big part of his life during his last three years. I like to think these were the best years of his life. I know they were his happiest years, having both of his daughters together.

Ruthie Shelton collection

TOGETHER AT LAST – "Little Carl" Shelton hugs both of his daughters, Elaine on the left and Ruthie on the right after they all finally reuinte after years of secrets.

Chapter 21.

The End of the Road

By the 1960s the gunfire had subsided, the smoldering ashes had gone out, and people began to breathe freely again in Fairfield, Illinois. In 1962, the legendary Frank Sinatra set in motion plans to make a movie about the "Shelton Gang," along with other members of the "Rat Pack."[109] Again, an amazing story to me as I was always a big fan of Sinatra's music.

The FBI files on Frank Sinatra also mention the movie that was never made. "Bureau memo 11/6/62 stated that Frank Sinatra, Dean Martin and Peter Lawford were reportedly heading a film syndicate which planned to make a movie entitled 'The End of the Road.'" The movie was to be about the Shelton-Birger gang war which terrorized southern Illinois during the 1920's.

The script was written, roles were cast. Frank Sinatra was going to play Big Carl Shelton! Members of the "Rat Pack" were also to be in it. Sinatra sent a production crew to Fairfield to cast some locals, but his "End of the Road," quickly came to a dead end as his plans were soon shot down. Earl Shelton would not hear of it and squashed all plans to make a movie about his family. I heard that Mabel Bell, Black Charlie's sister, caught wind of the planned movie and she too stepped in to have it stopped. Mabel was one tough woman and didn't take any grief off anyone. I was told by someone who grew up in Fairfield and asked to remain anonymous that "she

---

[109] Sept. 2, 1962. "Shelton Gang To Be Topic of Movie." *Southern Illinoisan* (Carbondale, Ill.).

didn't care what she said or who was around when she said it." Mabel Bell was also a known bootlegger. She kept her business going for years. After the Sheltons left Wayne County all the local bootleggers were kept supplied and financed by out-of-towners. There would be no movie about the Sheltons! At least not while the bootleggers were still alive.

Even with the my family out of the picture Wayne County's peace would once again be shattered. On June 17, 1965, Black Charlie was arrested for the murders of Betty Newton and Jerry Meritt. Their bodies were found in a house that had belonged to Courtney Meritt, Jerry's father. They had both been shot in the head and their bodies placed in the house, before it was set on fire. Harris' file with the Illinois State Police summarized the incident.

"On August 16, 1964, the Fairfield Fire Department received a call from the Courtney Meritt residence located on Delaware Street in Fairfield, that their rural farm home, located nine (9) miles southeast of Fairfield was on fire. Assistant Fire Chief Fred Book received this call and logged the call at 8:15 a.m. on August 16, 1964. Assistant Chief book notified firemen on call and when the Fairfield Fire Department arrived at the scene the house was completely leveled. Fire Chief Richard Miller smelled burning flesh and located two (2) partial torsos in the northwest downstairs bedroom. This area was sprayed continuously with water and Coroner Robert McNeill of Wayne County was notified."

"At approximately 10:30 a.m. on August 16, 1964, two (2) partial torsos were removed from the fire ruins by Coroner McNeill, Fire Chief Richard Miller, and Russell Dixon of the Dixon-Johnson Funeral Home in Fairfield, Illinois."

"Examination of the two (2) bodies found in the fire revealed suspicious holes in skull fragments which were believed to be bullet holes."

"Sheriff Eugene Leathers and State's Attorney Willard Pearce of Wayne County were notified."

There was a matter of three weeks that Black Charlie was known to be in Wayne County but law officers could not find him. I found it interesting that in line with keeping up with the Shelton boys years before, Black Charlie had a bunker built on his property in Pond Creek. It was sort of a bomb shelter. Built in the ground out of concrete block with an iron ladder attached to the wall to climb down in it. I know it was there because I've not only seen this bunker, but I've been in it! It was on a day a very informative Pond Creek native took me and my publisher Jon Musgrave on a tour to not just the Shelton sites but also Charlie Harris's and Virgil Vaughan's old stomping grounds. After visiting the bunker that I was fascinated with, I heard Jon say as we were walking away, "Ruthie never had a 'princess phase.'" I laughed as I thought to myself, "Truer words were never spoken."

When Black Charlie returned to Wayne County he went to the home of his older sister, Mabel Bell. She was five years older than her little brother and they were very close throughout their lives. Mabel's first husband Virney Bell died in 1925. About the same time Ross Suddarth, another farmer in the area, lost his wife. Soon he and Mabel started their own family. They didn't stay together long but a daughter came out of it, one that would change her name to Bell rather than Suddarth and would remain close to her Uncle Charlie 'til the end of his life.

Black Charlie was finally apprehended in Pond Creek. He was found in a vacant house at 5:30 in the morning. When the FBI agents surrounded the empty farmhouse, Black Charlie thought about it for a second, but he didn't go for the gun that lay near him. He simply answered, "I am Charlie Harris."

When his trial started there was a very unexpected observer there, my sister Elaine! Her dad Bill took her to the trial and walked her to the front row. When Black Charlie walked past them, Bill reached his hand out and they shook hands. "Dad said, 'Hi, Charlie, how are you?' Charlie said, 'Hi Bill.' Then dad said, 'Charlie, this is my daughter, Elaine,'" my sister recalled. Wayne County was and is a small place. There was no doubt Charlie knew who her biological father was. Bill just wanted it clear to Charlie that despite Elaine's genetics, she was *his* daughter. The message was received. No harm ever came to Elaine.

As the prosecution progressed government witnesses started to die. One of these was Charlie's nephew James Leo Bell, on October 10, 1966. He was the son of Charlie's sister Mabel Bell. This was just two months before a similar death occurred of a man that would cause the beginning of the end of my grandmother, Lillie's life.

The trial ran from August 21 to 25, 1967. Then the jury went out to deliberate the fate of Black Charlie Harris. It took only minutes for the jury to return with their verdict. *Guilty!* Charles Bryan Harris was sentenced to be in prison until the year 2015! But as things would always turn out in Black Charlie's favor, he was released from prison after serving only 14 years. It was a sentence that would have had him still in prison if he had lived until now, at the writing of this book. He was paroled from prison on February 3, 1981, and released from parole November 24, 1982. A far cry short of spending the rest of his life behind bars for the crimes he committed.

On June 20, 1988, Charles Bryan Harris peacefully fell asleep in death. He was simply resting on the couch, waiting for his supper, as he died from a brain hemorrhage. He was about to turn 92 years old at the time of his death. A quiet ending for such a monstrous life.

But it wasn't the end of the road, not for this war! In Fairfield on January 10, 1967, my grandmother, Lillie, died at 77 years old. She had remarried so she was no longer a Shelton, but a Miller. A grandmother I never got to know, never met, never even knew of, had died. Through my research I've since gotten to know a little bit more about her. She was a short woman, four foot something, and slightly stout. She always wore an apron pulled up and tied above her waist. Also, she dipped snuff. That's it. That's all I know about my grandmother. In all the research I did on my family I included her, but I found no one in Fairfield who knew or ever heard of her even though she lived most, if not all, of her life there in Wayne County.

It has been very difficult for me during this journey of discovery to find out that my little grandmother lived until I was six years old and I never got to meet her, but it's been even harder on Elaine. Finding out that her grandmother lived in the same town she grew up in, lived there and died there, has been very painful for her because she never knew about her. There was an old lady who used to watch Elaine walk home from school each day, she never spoke, never waved, just sat there on her porch and watched. Elaine has often wondered if this was Lillie.

Elaine and I sat together in the Fairfield library, looking at microfilm of old newspaper articles from the *Wayne County Press* for hours. We were trying to find out what happened to our grandmother. What we discovered that day was only the beginning.

Lillie worked as the live-in caretaker of Jesse Earl Kendal, who when he died at the age of 66 was listed on his death certificate as a common laborer. Lillie helped as caregiver because he was in a wheelchair. Kendal and Lillie had just moved into a rental house in Fairfield at #2 Talbert Court. On December 16, 1966, at 8 a.m. in the morning, Kendal died of a gunshot wound to the chest. According to the paper, "Authorities found Kendal dressed in long john underwear, his feet covered with thick athletic socks and house slippers... A single-shot 12 gauge shotgun was under his left leg, and there was a yardstick laying on top of the lower portions of his body... There was a leather glove on his left hand." Fairfield coroner Robert E. McNeill called it a "self inflicted gunshot wound."

This all took place in the months leading up to Black Charlie's big murder trial, and just two months after the similar death of Harris' nephew James Leo Bell, who was scheduled to be a witness against him. Bell was found dead of a shotgun blast to the throat at about 8 a.m. on October 10, 1966, lying with a shotgun by his side. He was wearing pajamas. A coroner's jury called his death self-inflicted as well although friends and family did not believe this.. What I found scary was that the name of the apartment owners was the same family name as the father of James Leo's sister. Another strange coincidence from a small county with lots of inter-related families.

Lillie called Dr. D. A. Gershenson's office and help was sent to the home. The paper said, "Mrs. Miller was in a state of shock when authorities arrived. She was taken by Dixon and Johnson ambulance to Memorial Hospital where she was admitted for treatment."

My extreme surprise came when I was able to obtain a copy of Kendall's death certificate. His sister signed it under "informant signature." His sister and I have the same married name, first and last!

Lillie stayed in the hospital for about three weeks. She did not recover from her trauma and was not able to go home. After three weeks of hospital care, Pop's brother, Little Earl, who worked as a truck driver out of Michigan at the time, drove to Fairfield to put his mother in a nursing home since she was unable to care for herself. Whatever she saw or heard on that cold, winter morning of December 19, 1966, caused this 77-year old woman, who had been the caregiver to a man 11 years younger than her, to no longer be able to care for herself!

But more tragedy was about to strike! The *Wayne County Press* reported, "Mrs. Miller was found unconscious in her bed in Fair Haven Nursing Home about 7:30 Monday morning and was rushed to the hospital at that time. She did not regain consciousness." Our grandmother Lillie, "died at 5:40 Tuesday evening at Memorial hospital." When we read these newspaper articles I turned to Elaine and said, "They took out our grandmother!" Before Little Earl was able to drive home, to Jacksonville, his mother, my father's mother, Elaine's and my grandmother was dead! She had been murdered!

Elaine looked at me and seriously said, "Is it safe for you to be here?" That was the one time during this experience that I really felt like I wanted to just close the door to this whole journey, go home to Florida and pretend that Pop never told me about his past. But I couldn't do that. I had to keep digging. No matter where it took me.

The newspaper went on to say, "Mrs. Miller had resided in Fairfield for 35 years. For Elaine's entire life she had a grandmother living alongside her in a town of 5,000 people where everybody knows everybody and she didn't know it.

Ruthie Shelton collection

ONE MORE MURDER – The murder of Ruthie's grandmother she never knew, Lillie (Myers) Biggs Shelton Miller not only remains unsolved, but has never before been made known.

An inquest was ordered by the coroner. From my home in Florida, with the help of some very thoughtful people in Fairfield, I was able to obtain a copy. During my research process I kept a post office box for the purpose of receiving Shelton information. I never used my home address. Pop's voice saying, "never let them know where we are," was always with me. I was expecting to receive a copy of Lillie's autopsy and the coroner's inquest, but I didn't expect what awaited me in that envelope!

I opened the post office box, got out the mail and returned to my car. I went through it and opened the mail relating to my Shelton research as I always did. After this experience my daughters told me not to open *any* mail until I was home. What I read when I opened that envelope made me sick physically. I sat in my car at the post office and cried. I called a coroner I know to see if what I thought I was reading was actually what it said. Unfortunately it was.

After her death on January 10, 1967, an autopsy was done in Fairfield by Coroner McNeill. Because of the results, my grandmother's stomach was sent to Indiana University Medical Center in Indianapolis, Indiana. They responded, "Report of general analysis for poisons in certain material from the body of Lillie Miller.

On January 13, 1967 we received by mail a package containing stomach and contents identified with the name Lillie Miller… The stomach contents were found to contain methyl alcohol in a concentration of 280 milligrams."

Methyl alcohol is also called "methanol." It is used in antifreeze. Methanol has a high toxicity when ingested. 30 ml is potentially fatal. A dose of 100-125 ml is fatal. That's about four ounces. The first symptoms include headache, dizziness, nausea, confusion, unconsciousness then death. This can take from 10 to 30 hours. Lillie had over twice this much, nine ounces, in her stomach. On her death certificate her cause of death was called "undetermined." I guess this was the new way to say death by "person or persons unknown."

I can only imagine someone coming quietly into her room in the nursing home, as she lay in bed sleeping, late at night or early in the morning. Was it only one person or did it take two brave big men, so one could hold down this little, old woman, while the other poured nine ounces of methanol down her throat. How she must have choked and gagged. I wonder what she thought about in those last moments of consciousness. Did she think about her children? Did she think about her grandchildren, about the granddaughters she never knew, Elaine and me? Did she even know about us? Neither of us ever knew about her.

Her funeral services were held at Nale's Funeral Home in Fairfield, Illinois. She was buried at Maple Hill Cemetery in Fairfield, Illinois, but not with the Sheltons. Little Earl, Pop, and some more of the family from Florida went to Fairfield for the funeral. I, of course, did not. I was six years old when my grandmother was poisoned. Elaine was 17.

Chapter 22.
The Worst Day

On February 12, 2009, "Little Carl" Shelton lost his battle with kidney cancer. Nell lost the love of her life. My family lost our "Pop." History lost the last living member of the Shelton Gang. He was surrounded by his family, holding his hands, telling him we love him. I put my hand on his chest as he took his last breath and I said, "We love you Pop."

I'll never forget the loss I felt as his last breath of life left his body. He was always there for me, from the moment I was born til the moment he died. Until a few years ago, shielding me from the knowledge of his former life as part of the Shelton Gang.

Only my strong faith and the love of my family got me through the next few days. Nell and I had to go to the funeral home to finalize the arrangements. Nell's daughter, Sadie, came with her and James and Missi brought me. Pop was so close with Sadie and her kids that we listed her as a daughter in Pop's obituary. I hated that we had to leave Elaine's name out, but she wasn't ready to be listed as a Shelton. This was very difficult for me but as I had dealt with things all my life, that was just how it had to be.

Pop had a military funeral to honor his time in the navy. The morning of the funeral, my kids were at my house, getting ready and doing whatever they could for us. I walked in and saw my children shooting pool. I said to them, "This is exactly how Pop would want it."

After the funeral when Pop's casket was about to be lowered into the ground, I saw the funeral director step up. He took one vase of flowers from all the arrangements that had been sent and pulled the flowers out. He handed one yellow rose to each family member and placed the rest on Pop's casket. How appropriate I thought. The last contact Pop had with those who loved him the most involved the flowers Elaine sent. His first daughter had the last say in his life. He will be buried with Elaine's roses forever. I love that!

They say we all handle our grief in different ways. My way of handling losing Pop was to throw myself into the research and writing of this book. I started out with the idea of writing a book about my family, the infamous Shelton Gang, when Pop and I would talk about the trip we made to Fairfield. All those people who came to the *Wayne County Press* office to meet Pop had stories about my family, good stories. Pop was sitting there, signing autographs and I was videotaping, but James was talking to people. He was just sitting, watching my hyperness as usual, and people gravitated toward him. He has that quiet, calm quality about him. He's easy to talk to. So that's what so many people did. They talked to him. They told him, and me when I was still, about how my uncles helped their families in difficult times. This gave me a lot to think about.

I started by running a letter to the editor in the *Wayne County Press*, asking for the "good Shelton stories." I received several letters in the mail from people who read my request and wanted to share what they knew about my family. I always took the letters out to Pop's and read them to him. Sometimes he would remember the people spoken of, sometimes he could even add to what had been written.

I heard from a lot of people who had never spoken out about the Sheltons before, maybe out of fear or maybe they just never felt the need. I guess I'm in a very unusual, if not privileged position, being Carl Shelton's daughter, and many people have been very willing to share secrets – some very long hidden secrets – with me. Many times the information came with the addendum – don't tell where you got this information. It is for this reason that much of the information in this book being shared with you doesn't come with precise source details. I simply cannot divulge where I got the information.

When I put together all the information I received about the "good" side of the Sheltons it would have filled a small pamphlet! As Pop told me more about his past, and as I did more research, research that could only be accomplished by a descendent of the family, I realized I needed to tell the good as well as the criminal side. When Jon Musgrave told me he wanted to publish my book he thought I also needed to tell my part of the story, my journey in learning about my family. So this gave my writing a new dimension that helped me work through my emotions as I was learning about and coming to terms with my family's past.

Along with all the research I've done I have met a lot of wonderful people. Some of them happen to be related to me. I came to find out I have cousins still in the Fairfield area, distant cousins, but still family. I got to know some of my family long distance but I wanted to meet everyone personally. One day I had the idea to have a Shelton family reunion in Fairfield. I put the idea online and the next thing I knew it was being planned! In August 2010 we had the first Shelton Family Reunion at the Leo French Park in Fairfield, just across the road from the cemetery where so many of the Sheltons are buried. There were about 70 people, a good time and a ton of great food there.

I had requested guns be brought so we could take pictures but that didn't work out, something about being within city limits. I don't think that ever bothered the older generation of Sheltons! Then one of my cousins went to his truck and got me a bullet. So in every picture I'm holding up a 9 mm bullet!

When did the war end? I don't really know. I'd like to think it ended that day Pop rode back into Fairfield, not wanting any trouble, just a dad wanting to show his daughter around his hometown. Maybe it hasn't ended yet. So many people don't want to tell what they know about my uncle's deaths out of fear of retaliation, how could we say for sure that it has ended. The murders are still unsolved. I think the final phase should be the solving of the murders, including that of my little grandmother.

Was Pop ever actually kidnapped? Not that I could find out. I think his delusions in the hospital, what now seems like a lifetime ago, were partly from his horrific experiences in the navy and partly from the fear he lived with of being discovered for the last fifty years.

That fear or paranoia passed down through the generations. I've raised my children with lessons of "what to do if..." long before it was the popular thing to do. What to do if there's a shooting – duck and take cover. What to do if there's a bomb – run, keep running, and don't look back. What to do if you're surfing and the "wrong" planes fly over (we live in a navy town) – take cover under your board. I was raised with a lot of paranoia, but as Elaine says, "It's not paranoid if it's real!"

When Pop started revealing to me the truth about his past he was reluctant to tell me the whole story. He sort of sugarcoated everything.

"What's the difference between gangsters and bootleggers?" he asked me. "Gangsters kill people, bootleggers bootleg. We were bootleggers."

But as he saw that his past life made no difference in how I viewed him, he started to really open up to me, and tell me everything. No more sugarcoating, just his past life. What he did, he viewed as, simply put, his life. He grew up with gangsters for uncles, came out of the navy to a job waiting for him with his uncles, and was given anything he wanted. Pop was the baby in the family and he was spoiled. He also had the Shelton temper. It wasn't until many years later that he learned to control it.

This whole experience, my journey of discovery it's been called, has had life altering effects for me. When we were in Fairfield with Pop, we loved the hometown feeling. James, Krystin and I visited the area several times after that day. Every time we enjoyed being there more. Finally we decided to make a more permanent visit. We bought twenty acres with an old farmhouse in nearby Albion, Edwards County, Illinois, the next county over from Wayne County.

This was the greatest adventure we've ever had. We loved that farm. We had horses, dogs, cats, (every animal that needed a home came to us), dirt bikes, four-wheelers, and the best neighbors we ever could have dreamed of! My neighbors often laughed at the "Florida girl" trying to survive life in the rural country of the Midwest. It's quite different than life in Jacksonville, even in the country parts of Florida, especially when it snowed!

While we were there I only used my married name. Pop was so worried about what could happen if the "wrong people" found out I was "Little Carl's daughter. Only my closest friends knew who my dad was. And if anyone else knew, they were polite enough not to mention it.

We came back home every few months, Pop's health was deteriorating and he wanted me with him and Nell for his doctor visits. After nearly three years we sold our farm and moved back home to Jacksonville. It was good timing because Pop and Nell really needed me at that point.

I feel that I am greatly privileged in that I truly have two homes. I was born and raised in Jacksonville and this will always be my home. The beach is in my blood. But I have another home now, the place my where family settled looking for good farmland, the land my dad grew up on. I can understand why my family didn't want to leave their land. It was "home!"

Uncle Earl once said that his land was, "where I belong. On my own property."

I know why Uncle Earl wanted to go back and farm his land, even after all the violence that caused him to take his family away. It was his home, not the houses, not any kind of buildings, but the land. The land becomes part of you, and Pond Creek will always be part of me.

Ruthie Shelton collection

SAYING GOODBYE – "Little Carl" Shelton's casket at the cemetery in Jacksonville bears the yellow roses from his eldest daughter Elaine.

1/1/200

Chapter **23.**
Telling All

When I began this process, this "journey of discovery" to find out all I could about my family, it seemed very simple. I thought it was going to be easy to write this book about them, and later after my publisher was in the picture, to write about my part of the journey at his suggestion. But I was wrong. Very wrong! The writing of my book has been one of the most difficult things I've ever tried to accomplish. It seemed simple enough in the beginning, you collect all the facts, organize the dates, then just put it on paper.

But at some point my research took me past the names, dates and facts of this story. It took me right into the living rooms of the people telling me. I could no longer look at it from a distance and just report. Now I was in it and I had to, not just think, but I had to feel. The "box in my head" which locked away facts so many years before had moved into my heart, many times resulting in things I didn't want to feel. I empathized with the people whose lives I had entered, and shared what they were feeling when they were communicating with me. These were no longer just names on a website or on a page sent to me in the mail, these people were living with families they cared about.

I've looked into their eyes, even the baby blue eyes of someone my great uncle Earl loved dearly and I realized this is more than a few facts and dates on paper, a lot more. This is the history of the lives, good or bad, that have led to the lives these dear people are living today, people that I've had the greatest privilege of coming to know. Some of these people loved my family as their own. Some of them hated my family, with every reason, in my opinion, to do so, and yet they willingly shared their secrets with me. Some of them very painful, lifelong held secrets. With the sharing of their most deeply hidden thoughts was always a consideration of my feelings. Sometimes with the words, "I don't want to hurt you but…," and they continued their stories that had been carefully concealed for a lifetime as if they had to be told now or they would be lost forever.

It's been very painful to me, coming to grips with what my dad's former life really was. The fact that I never knew, never was *allowed* to know, what my heritage is, was always something I had to deal with on my own. No one could understand how I felt not having any "background," because their families didn't keep them "hidden." It hurt me when teachers looked at me like I didn't want to do an assignment when I *couldn't* do the assignment because my dad's past didn't exist to me.

So many years have been lost between me and my sister, Elaine. Years we could have known each other, raised our kids together, she could have been there for me when my mother decided to "give me away." Yes, as I reflect on this "journey of discovery," I've been on these last few years, it has been difficult. Not just finding out about the glitz and glamour surrounding my dad because he was the nephew of famous gangsters, or finding out that my dad personally knew people I had always admired, or at least knew about, but never told me. It's been the more personal side of things I've learned. My uncles were, to say the least, bootleggers, gangsters, thieves, pimps, murderers. My elderly grandmother, that I never even was allowed to meet, was murdered in her bed at a nursing home after the horrific death of the man in her care. And there have been some facts my dad told me about but when I look at them on paper it was very hard to take.

There has been one part of my dad's life that I've agonized over whether to tell or not. As I sit here looking at my keyboard, trying to invent the right, the proper way to tell it, I feel the knife stabbing me in my stomach that I've felt many times while I've been learning about my dad's past. But this time it's not what I'm learning that's causing it, because I already know, it's the question of "should I tell or not?" If I don't tell all about my dad, people may never discover the whole truth about him. Who he really was and all the things he did in his former life. If I don't tell I can go on with my life pretending these things never happened.

But if I don't tell it, here and now, then my whole book is a fraud, and not one word I've written is worth a hill of beans. I finally made the decision to hit it head on.

This is very painful for me to have to write. And I know it will be even more painful for my family to read, but it has to be done.

On Wednesday, December 27, 1950, my dad was convicted in Indiana on a morals charge. His accuser was a minor girl. When the trial finally came, his wife Dorothy sat beside him in court. They were seen whispering to each other. If Dorothy had the least doubt about his innocence she would *not* have been there! He pled guilty and was fined $400 and court costs with time served. He told me emphatically, *I did not do it!*" He said he was not guilty but pled guilty just to get it over with. He had already spent five months in the county jail, another month at the state penal farm wouldn't be that bad. Apparently it was a plea deal. In exchange the state dropped the more serious charge of kidnapping. He did not know why the charges were made against him. But I do.

I discovered, much too late to tell my dad, that someone paid $25,000 for him to be arrested and have these charges brought against him. Twenty-five thousand dollars was a lot of money in 1950 and someone wanted my dad out of the way badly enough to spend that kind of money to make it happen. My information came from someone who had every reason to hate the Sheltons, yet this secret was shared with me. My dad was a hothead. He was also a sharp-shooter. He had already declared openly on the square of Fairfield, that he would take care of his uncles' murderers himself, his way. He was a loose cannon that couldn't be controlled so he was removed from the situation.

What my dad failed to tell me about was why the Indiana charges against him were so easily believed. This is the part I find so difficult for me to accept, and even more difficult for me to write. A few months earlier he had previously been charged with molesting a young girl in Fairfield. In November 1949, just a couple of months after the drive-by shooting at Little Earl's house, Pop was accused of taking indecent liberties with a minor girl at the local theater. Although a grand jury indicted him for the crime, at trial the judge approved a defense attorney's motion to direct the jury to acquit him on the "grounds that evidence was lacking."

In an era when an eighth grade education was considered enough and the age of consent was younger than what many realize today, teen-age girls (and sometimes younger) were often targeted. Going through the list of gang members associated with my uncles and Charlie Birger it's not uncommon to find statutory rape charges, or stories where charges should have been filed. A daughter of Jack Skelcher, one of my uncles' top lieutenants from the earliest days of the gang, once told another researcher the story of Jack instructing his children's babysitter to immediately leave the house by the back door if she ever saw his co-workers in the gang arrive out front. It was for her protection.[110] Birger all but preyed on teen girls. The "blonde bombshell" whom Gary DeNeal interviewed back in the 1970s for his biography of Birger, *A Knight of Another Sort*, though never identified by name, was likely just 15 or 16 when she started as hostess and exotic dancer at Shady Rest.[111] It was simply a part of that world back then. At this point in my dad's life he was a full-out gangster and had that mentality. If the prevailing attitude of the environment around him altered my dad's moral compass to the point that he thought child molestation was an acceptable behavior, then I am appalled and disgusted. The Shelton family was being murdered one by one, their houses were being bombed and burned down, and yet Big Earl Shelton wouldn't leave the Midwest until his nephew was safely out of jail.

On the day my dad was released Uncle Earl picked him up and the family headed to Florida. My dad's first wife Dorothy, refused to leave her home, and she and their little girl Elaine stayed in Fairfield. She filed for a divorce, which was finalized on October 16, 1951, and she got full custody of Elaine. On June 28, 1954, Dorothy had her daughter Elaine Shelton's name legally changed.

---

[110] Jim Smith. Jan. 14, 2011. Presentation on Jack Skelcher for the Herrin Area Historical Society at the Herrin City Library.

[111] While Mr. DeNeal promised not to reveal his source's name, and to date, has not, my publisher believes he has uncovered her true identity through other documents. The woman in question was born Jan. 10, 1910, which would have made her 16 during the final year of Shady Rest's existence. It's not clear from *A Knight of Another Sort* exactly when she started working for Birger. If she started in 1925 she would have been just 15.

Chapter 24.

Our Lives Changed

For the last few years I have been on the adventure of a lifetime. As I began the search for information about my family I had no idea what lay ahead. I was able to learn about a farmer and his wife whose love for each other was unbendable regardless of the hardships they faced in life. This would be my great grandparents, Ben and Agnes Shelton. To know that the beginning of my journey would be a true love story really warms my heart. After all the dysfunction I was raised with, to find loving roots in my heritage, is more than I could ask for. It somehow makes up for all the negative side of the story I would discover. My great-grandfather Ben died of cancer before my great uncles started to be killed off. My great grandmother Agnes, never remarried. She stayed devoted to her "Ben" and her children for the rest of her life.

I've been asked how my experience has changed me. It has definitely changed my life in that I now have my sister, Elaine, as part of my life. This has given me more happiness than I could ever possibly express. That little "princess" in the picture I found as a small child is now one of my closest family members and one of my dearest friends.

But it's changed me in other ways, too. I once very much resented my mother for many of the things she did and the ways she treated me as a child and as an adult. I tried to stay in touch with her over the years, to call and see if she needed anything, if she was well. I tried to take my children to see her. She refused all of my efforts to have her as part of me and my children's lives. I had not seen her in 26 years by her choice, not mine. I am a Shelton and I chose to have my dad in my life. Because of those two elements she chose to take herself out of mine.

After finding out the truth about my dad's past and what much of my mother's life must have been like, I now only feel an incredible amount of sadness toward her and her life. I am truly glad she did not find out about my research and plans to write this book. I know reading these pages would have caused her tremendous pain. I'm also glad I did not finish my book before she died. For all the pain she endured because of the Sheltons, their fault or not, learning that I was writing a book about them would have been too much for her. My mother died January 4, 2011, in Jacksonville, Florida from heart failure due to lymphoma.

I was researching online to see if Uncle Roy had any grandchildren. In searching for his obituary, I happened to find my mother's death certificate. That was how I found out my mother had died.

I went to see my older brother after I learned of my mother's death. For various reasons my relationship with him hasn't been any better than with my mother. When they divorced I got Pop, he got Mom. As we talked we compared stories. Putting them together gave us a whole new overview of how we were raised. Nothing was as it seemed at the time. He had half of the truth and I had the other half. It took us coming together to realize what had been done to us, to our relationship, to our lives. During the conversation I asked him if he knew about Pop's past. "I knew about his surgery," he said.

"No, I mean before he came to Florida?"

To my extreme surprise he responded, "Oh, you mean about him being a gangster. I've known since elementary school."

I could hardly believe my ears. How could he possibly have known? Then he told me, "I was quiet, and I listened."

That few years difference in age was all that mattered. He was young enough to hide, but old enough to listen. Now he, Elaine and I have lost all of our parents in death.

There have been several "defining moments" for both Elaine and myself since the concept of this book. The one that really stands out to me for my sister was at the funeral of her dad that raised her, Bill Garrett. She was standing by his casket with her siblings. The line of mourners was long. An older gentlemen stepped up to give his condolences to the family. He looked at Elaine and then asked the question that had *never* been openly asked, "Are you 'Little Carl' Shelton's daughter?" There was a time even the mention of the Shelton name in public would have left bought Elaine and myself shaking in our boots.

A lifetime of thoughts and feelings rushed through Elaine in an instant! She reacted from her gut. The gut instinct that for so many years kept her safe, kept her hidden from any and all things Shelton. But this time it was different. With all the confidence and straight forwardness a Shelton can muster she stood up straight and looked right into his baby blue eyes. Her reply, a very simple, "*Yes, I am!*"

He was moved along the line by family members. I spoke to him later and I asked him why he did that. His answer to me was, "I just wanted to know" if that was Little Carl's daughter all grown up.

That was Elaine's "defining moment" in this experience we have shared. The moment she realized how much she had changed. She no longer had to hide who she was. For the first time ever she could ignore a lifetime of deeply entrenched warnings.

I haven't had my "defining moment" yet. I've hidden behind my dad's name for all this time. I've only used the Shelton name for my research and in meeting people. Very soon now, this book will be published and I will be in Fairfield, Illinois, for the release. With my husband at my side I will no longer be able to hide under the cover of the Shelton name. I'll just be me.

Another way this experience has change my life is that I now have a second home, a very special area in the Midwest. The place I so longed to see all those years ago when Pop told me about his past life, Wayne County, Illinois. Just a tiny dot on a map, it has become a very important part of my life. I feel the same love for the land that my great Uncle Earl felt.

Also, I have been greatly blessed to have added to my life many new family members and great friends through this journey of discovery. My great-grandfather Benjamin Marsh Shelton came from a very large family. His brothers and sisters also had big families. I've had the great privilege of meeting many of my cousins and I have become very close to some of them. They have been very supportive and helpful to me while I have been researching our family.

But most of all, this journey I've been on, for over three years now, has given me a greater sense of self-confidence, and a more enhanced awareness of who I am. I no longer feel like I am simply an alien from a distant planet with no connections to anyone on this earth. I know where I came from. I know where my family came from. I feel, more than ever, I know who I am. Working through all the emotions I've had since learning of my dad's true past has left me with only one feeling, that of gratitude! I'm so thankful for the life I now have. And thanks to Pop, I've had a chance to live my dream, and in the words of my Pop, who always faced every adventure with the words, "Let's do it!"

I did!

Acknowledgements

I want to thank the people who answered my request for the good stories about the Sheltons. Pop got a lot of joy when I shared them with him.

I would like to thank the relatives of the people I wrote about who shared their families stories with me.

I especially want to thank my cousins, some of them I've only met because of my research. They have spent long hours researching in person, making copies, sending me information, doing the legwork for me when I couldn't be there physically to do it myself.

My good friend, Glenda Young, has been a tremendous help to me right from the start. She is always there for me, no matter what the need. Thank you Glenda.

Thank you to the volunteers at the Hanna House Museum. Their work in general, and more specifically for me, on the Shelton exhibit and files goes above and beyond.

To Tommy Matthews, thank you for running my letters that began my quest for information and for making Pop feel like a hometown hero. He thought a lot of you.

I also want to thank my hard-working, patient with me, publisher Jon Musgrave.

I want to say a huge thank you to my family. My children, Missi, J.C., Jenny and Krystin have supported my dream emotionally and physically. Doing hours of research online, hitting the trail with me to talk to people, digging through old library files, and filling in for me on the home front so I could devote my time to my book. My children are proud of their mama and that means the world to me.

If I haven't said thank you enough to my loving, wonderfully supportive husband, here it is. James, you have stuck by me through this whole experience, even though you have been battling your own life threatening illness. You have been by my side through all the emotional ups and downs of this journey I've been on. You have given of yourself so I could focus on my goal. You have pushed me ahead when I have slowed down. You have told me since day one that I could do it. Thank you.

And to Elaine, my sister, my friend – I am so happy we have shared this experience together. You have been with me every step of the way through this journey of discovery. Thank you for truly being my sister.

Ruthie Shelton collection
THE JOURNEY – The author Ruthie Shelton as a young woman riding her dirt bike in Florida.

Bibliography

A Note about our Sources

As Ruthie explained earlier in the book many of her sources were stories told by her father "Little Carl" Shelton and other relatives. Often these stories did not come with dates or bibliographic references. Where permitted she identified by name or position the person providing her with information. Many did not want their names used.

Footnotes throughout the book cover topics either learned through research, or added to help verify or date the oral traditions told to Ruthie. Although rarely directly sourced the writers are deeply indebted to the previous work on the Shelton Gang by Taylor Pensoneau and Bill Adams, as well as Gary DeNeal and Paul Angle. In addition the original documents provided by Ancestry.com and NewspaperArchive.com proved critical to this work.

Books

Bill Adams. 2005. *The Shelton Gang: They Played In Peoria and the Played War in "Bloody Williamson County."* Xlibris Corporation.

Paul M. Angle. 1952. *Bloody Williamson: A Chapter in American Lawlessness.* 1952. New York: Alfred A. Knopf.

George Galligan and Jack Wilkinson. 1927, Reprinted 1985. *In Bloody Williamson.* Marion, Ill.: Williamson County Historical Society.

E. Bishop Hill. 1927, Rep. 2006. *Complete History of Southern Illinois Gang War: The True Story of Southern Illinois Gang Warfare.* Marion, Ill.: Williamson County Historical Society.

Rudolph Lasker. 1925. *Bloody Herrin.* Washington, D.C.: Patriotic Publishers. The Chicago Historical Society has a copy of this rare pamphlet, appropriately dressed in a blood-red cover. Gary DeNeal wrote an introduction for the pamphlet which he reprinted in the Vol. 23, No. 1, edition of *Springhouse* magazine. (Note: The cover states it is Vol. 22, No. 6.)

Ralph Johnson and Jon Musgrave. 2010. *Secrets of the Herrin Gangs*. Marion, Ill. IllinoisHistory.com.

Margaret N. O'Shea. 1974. *Oldham Paisley: A Community Editor and His Newspapers, Marion Daily Republican and Marion Weekly Leader, 1915-1970*. Privately published.

[Homer Butler and Oldham Paisley]. 1927, Reprinted 1994. *The Life Story of Charlie Birger: History of the Crimes of The Birger Gang*. Marion, Ill.: The Illinois Book Co. (original); Williamson County Historical Society (reprint).

Chatland Parker. 1923. Reprint, 1979. *The Herrin Massacre*. Marion, Ill.: Williamson County Historical Society.

Taylor Pensoneau. 2002. *Brothers Notorious*. New Berlin, Ill.: Downstate Publications.

Taylor Pensoneau. 2010. *Dapper & Deadly: The True Story of Black Charlie Harris*. New Berlin, Ill.: Downstate Publications.

Curtis G. Small. 1970. *Mean Old Jail*. Harrisburg, Ill.: Register Publishing Co.

Articles

Gary DeNeal. Aug. 2002. "Springhouse Ink." *Springhouse*. 19:4. 3. In his regular column DeNeal mentions learning of the old stories about Charlie Birger and the gangsters from his grandfather Guy DeNeal.

Brocton Lockwood. Dec. 2001. "Delos L. Duty: Williamson County's Bravest Man." *Springhouse*. 18:6. 6-19.

Herbert K. Russell. Aug. 2002. "The Silent Source of Bloody Williamson." *Springhouse*. 19:4. 13-16. Focuses on Hal W. Trovillion's role in Herrin during the 1920s and later as a source for Paul Angle in his book Bloody Williamson.

Hal W. Trovillion. Spring 2003. "Persuading God Back to Herrin." *Springhouse*. 20:1.

Index